Walking
Hadrian's
Wall

Walking Hadrian's Wall

A Memoir of a Father's Suicide

Bob Royalty

SHANTI ARTS PUBLISHING
BRUNSWICK, MAINE

Walking Hadrian's Wall
A Memoir of a Father's Suicide

Published by Shanti Arts Publishing

Interior and cover design by Shanti Arts Designs

All photographs, including that on the cover, were taken
by the author and are used with his permission.

Shanti Arts LLC | 193 Hillside Road
Brunswick, Maine 04011 | shantiarts.com

Printed in the United States of America

This book recounts memories of events that occurred
during years in the author's earlier life. It is based on his
best recollection of incidents, locales, and conversations. To
protect privacy, some names and identifying characteristics
have been changed.

ISBN: 978-1-951651-90-9 (softcover)
ISBN: 978-1-951651-91-6 (ebook)

Library of Congress Control Number: 2021940317

*Dedicated to all families whose lives
have been affected by depression and suicide*

CONTENTS

ACKNOWLEDGMENTS

This project would never have started without Dwight Watson's invitation to give the LaFollette lecture at Wabash College in 2016. I thank Dwight for this honor and the College for supporting my travel to Hadrian's world in England, Rome, Spain, and Provence over the course of writing this book. Nor would you be reading this if Christine Cote had not accepted the manuscript for Shanti Arts Publishing. Her fine editing has made this a better book.

Many friends and colleagues offered advice, support, or much-welcomed encouragement along the way. I owe a debt of gratitude to Roz Foster, now at Frances Goldin Literary Agency, who helped me turn my draft into a narrative. I also want to acknowledge Joy Castro, Gregory Erickson, Celeste Fine of Park and Fine Literary Agency, Marcus Folch, Eric Freeze, Marc Hudson, Andrew Jacobs, Sophie Lambert of C&W Literary Agency, Corey Mesler, Michele Pittard, and Blair Kutrow and Vic Roberts.

My family has been supportive throughout this project, from having two wonderful traveling companions in Anne and Ginna during three days of the walk to my mother, sister, and Nolen coming to hear the lecture. The story is painful for all of us. But I think opening this up again after twenty-five years has been healing as well.

BIRDS SEEN WHILE WALKING HADRIAN'S WALL

1	European Goldfinch	23	Eurasian Jackdaw
2	European Robin	24	Black-legged Kittiwake
3	Eurasian Blue Tit	25	Common Tern
4	Willow Tit	26	Mew Gull
5	Willow Warbler	27	Black-headed Gull
6	Eurasian Blackbird	28	Ring-necked Pheasant
7	Common Chaffinch	29	Common Chiffchaff
8	Barn Swallow	30	Yellowhammer
9	Song Thrush	31	Spotted Flycatcher
10	Eurasian Magpie	32	Eurasian Skylark
11	White Wagtail	33	Eurasian Oystercatcher
12	Grey Heron	34	Eurasian Kestrel
13	Red Kite	35	Eurasian Curlew
14	Common Buzzard	36	Peregrine Falcon
15	Whinchat	37	Eurasian Siskin
16	European Stonechat	38	Grey Wagtail
17	Great Crested Grebe	39	Common Redpoll
18	Eurasian Coot	40	Great Tit
19	Eurasian Moorhen	41	Coal Tit
20	Greylag Goose	42	Eurasian Linnet
21	Tufted Duck	43	Eurasian Reed Warbler
22	Carrion Crow	44	Common Swift

MAP

Hadrian's Wall Walk

These are the places where the author stopped while walking Hadrian's Wall.

1. Wallsend
2. The Big Lamp Brewery
3. The Miners Arms
4. Carraw Bed and Breakfast
5. Beggar Bog
6. Broomshaw Hill Farm B&B
7. Park Broom Lodge
8. Boustead Hill
9. Bowness on Solway

map by Bob Royalty

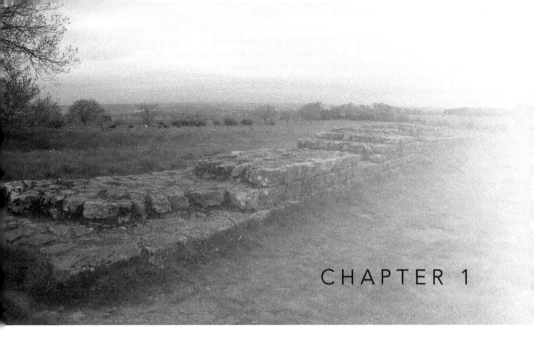

CHAPTER 1

KITTIWAKES

～ Nesters

F ive years before he put a garden hose in the exhaust pipe of his car, pulled it through the window of the driver's seat, and started the car, I stood next to my father out in the large field in front of the main house at Stillwaters Farm in Pine Mountain Valley, Georgia, while he explained how to use the wood splitter in his typical, step-by-step way. I was twenty-six and he was fifty-four. My parents did not want me to drive the old 1950s-era Ford tractor, only the lawn tractor, even though I was better with machines, especially boats, than him. More than once my father got stuck on the tractor while bush-hogging the fields, which weren't really farm fields unless a friend or neighbor put horses out there (and once, a zebra). I remember thinking to myself that morning in 1986, *I'll remember this moment when he's dead.*

There was no sign whatsoever that he would commit suicide. My younger brother had been killed in a car accident five years earlier—they were all drunk, the driver survived—and my sister got divorced the following year. But I don't think those life blows, hard as they were, caused my father to take his own life. I think someone considers suicide because of what's going inside their own life, not because of what's happening with others, not even their closest family.

We talk about freedom all the time, but we are never truly free, free of memories, pain, family entanglements, of burdens that we carry our entire life. For ten days I tasted freedom while walking the length of Hadrian's Wall in northern England, from the gritty old city of Newcastle upon Tyne on the east coast to the peaceful fields west of Carlisle and the Firth of Solway on the Scottish border. Even though we all carry many burdens, I felt free. This is the story of the walk, of me and my father, of burdens and freedom.

My father committed suicide at his Atlanta home—the center of our family life until that day, the 13th of May 1991, and where I lived from age eight to eighteen. This was twenty-five years before I left for England to walk the wall. It wasn't until after I had planned the walk that I realized it would happen on this anniversary.

Why was I walking Hadrian's Wall? Because I wanted to, is the simplest explanation. This started when I taught in England for a semester and visited the wall for a day with my wife, Anne, and my brother-in-law Brian while we were driving from Durham to Lindisfarne. I was fifty-three at the time and enjoying my second sabbatical from teaching at a small liberal arts college in Indiana where I had taught for fifteen years. Brian told me that people walked the length of the wall "as a thing to do," and I was immediately hooked on the idea.

I had visited Hadrian's Wall once before, but both visits in a car seemed inadequate; I didn't feel I had gotten the full experience. I wanted to wake up and go to sleep along the wall, not drop in and out like a tourist who just saw ruins of forts and car parks. A car trip felt confined, and I wanted the freedom of walking the length of the wall alone. It was a challenge, something to prove. I also knew that I had been invited to give the prestigious annual humanities lecture within a year or two after returning from sabbatical. As a professor of early Christianity—that is, Christians in the ancient Roman world—talking about a walk along the wall felt like a great way to present my research to a wide audience in a way that someone like my mother could understand. And the next year I would turn fifty-four, which meant in the due course of things I would turn fifty-five. Turning fifty was a blast—parties and celebrations for months, a special trip to Costa Rica to do a lot of birding. I found myself approaching fifty-five in a more pensive mood. Not depressed or sad, but thinking more about benchmarks and goals I want to accomplish next. I've never liked the phrase "bucket list," but I guess I thought the walk along the wall would be on my bucket list. It was a thing to do, like a hundred-mile bike ride. But it turned out to be much more than that.

Back on campus the following year for the fall semester, with a full teaching load once again, I started planning for the trip to walk the wall. For a professor, "planning" means "finding money," and I was fortunate to get a couple of grants to travel to England to walk the wall the following May; this would be preparation for my big campus talk coming up the next fall.

During the fall semester, I also trained for and rode the Hilly Hundred bicycle ride, a two-day ride in the beautiful rolling hills north and west of Bloomington, Indiana, in Owen and Brown Counties, where the film *Breaking Away* was set. The Hilly is a Midwest institution with riders attending from New York and California as well as neighboring states, often arriving by bicycle. During the many hours of training in the saddle, I thought a lot about the lecture, the themes and ideas I would explore, the ways in which I would wow the crowd and bring them to their feet! I had it all planned out.

During winter break that year, celebrating our first Christmas back at home after the sabbatical abroad, I realized that it had been twenty-five years since we learned how sick my father was in 1990. He died the following May. I would walk the wall on the twenty-fifth anniversary of his suicide. I began to think differently about the lecture and the experience of walking the wall. This wasn't just a "bucket list" walk anymore, a shallow physical challenge to prove myself at fifty-five, but a walk into a painful period in my own past of twenty-five years ago, a walk into my father's death and our life together. That's the story I am telling in this book, a story of a walk across England and a walk into my past. A walk into the unknown. I would have a guidebook and map, but I really didn't know where I was going.

Planning continued through January, when we figured out how Anne and our daughter, Ginna, could join me for part of the walk. I made all the reservations for travel and lodging for the nine days while walking Hadrian's Wall. My fifty-fifth birthday in February was mostly about buying new equipment: a pack, boots, clothes, a good rain jacket. Training started in March, and I began hiking with a fully loaded backpack in April.

We flew to Europe on Sunday, May 15. The Sunday before, I gave the flowers at church in memory of my father, which I've done before, but this time the bulletin announcement said, "Flowers today are given to the Glory of God and in memory of Robert M. Royalty, 1933–1991, and for all families who are afflicted by depression and suicide, from Bob and Anne Royalty." I had never mentioned his suicide publicly before that day. Of course people knew when it happened, and classmates and professors in graduate school at Yale and everyone in Atlanta who came to the funeral or was close to me at the time knew. But people forget. And as we moved on from graduate school, first to Stanford University and then to Indiana, I didn't introduce myself as "Bob Royalty whose father committed suicide." I told a few people, when appropriate, but not many and maybe only two at my college. No one knew outside of my family and a few close friends. I had never mentioned my father's suicide publicly, but after twenty-five years it seemed like time.

A week later, we left. I'm a nervous flyer but not usually when we travel to Europe because for some reason I think that larger airplanes are less likely than smaller ones to fall back down after take-off, which of course makes no sense. Since my job includes generous research and conference funds, I've been to England or Europe almost every summer for the last fifteen years. But the weekend before I left to walk Hadrian's Wall, I was a nervous wreck. I went back to REI, for maybe the eleventh time, for no good reason; I really didn't need any more socks. While driving around Zionsville and Indianapolis, I played with my brand new GoPro, shooting perhaps the worst videos anyone has ever taken. I loaded and repacked my backpack over and over. My walking poles and knee brace had to go in the extra suitcase for now—if airport security let me carry them on at all—since the poles could whack someone on the airplane. And there wasn't room in my backpack for the knee brace because, well, it was for my knee.

The brace was a legacy of hurting my right knee just a month before. This was to be my first backpacking trip since I was a teenage Boy Scout, and the training reminded me that I was fifty-five, not fifteen. I began training during spring break in March, just over two months before departure, slowly increasing mileage. The first weekend of April I took the longest hike to date with a full pack around Eagle Creek Park in Indianapolis and ended with right knee pain. I hiked again the next Tuesday, which turned out to be maybe the worst day at work in my career (but more on that later), and by Wednesday the pain was severe. I hobbled around campus and climbed the stairs to my office—in an old building with no elevator—slowly and painfully and as infrequently as possible. No one in my department seemed to care in the least. I had to scale back training for most of April, during which I made two visits to orthopedists, got a steroid shot, and started physical therapy. I didn't try the pack again for two weeks. There were a lot of dark moods during this time, only a few weeks before the walk was scheduled to start. I was scared I wouldn't be able to do it. Flights and lodging were booked, but I wasn't sure my dream would even start, let alone finish. And then the lecture would flop—no one wants to hear about a magnificent walk that didn't happen. So the knee brace had to go with me. While the shot and the therapy seemed to help, enough for two weeks of full training before flying to England, I had no way of knowing if it would hold up over 100 miles of walking. I hoped it would. But I had no idea how steep the trail would actually turn out to be.

Anne and I were flying to England together, and Ginna would join Anne later in London after finishing her exams, whence they would spend a day or two in Liverpool, then catch a train to find me, hopefully on schedule and able to continue a fourth day of walking. The dining room table was covered with our "Europe gear": pounds and euros, bird books, Oyster cards for the Tube, converters for phone and tablet, various travel gadgets such as a drying line for clothes to use in hotel rooms, the little green bags from REI that I always use overseas for small equipment. This is usually the fun time of anticipation, but I was jittery on Friday and Saturday. By Sunday, departure day, I couldn't concentrate and could barely keep still. Finally, I took a Xanax about an hour before we left for the airport. These had been prescribed for me a few years before when I was going through a period of extreme anxiety worrying about our son, who was going through a rough patch of depression. With my father's history, he had worried me a lot. The doctor who prescribed the pills asked if I was a nervous flyer, and when I said yes she answered, "You're going to love them." For a while I was taking one or two a day until a different doctor warned me about addiction. I just stopped cold for eighteen months until this day. Ginna's friend Taylor, who had finished her semester, was going with us to the airport to take our car home, but I drove there. That was when I realized the pill might have been a mistake. Anne offered to drive, but I foolishly held on. We made it, and Taylor took off with our car and to take care of our dog while we were away. Air Canada was a somewhat disastrous check-in (the pill helped!) but we got through in time for a meal. Anne had a glass of wine with her lunch, but I was pretty woozy and had tea.

It's too short a flight to London to get much sleep, and we were tired on arrival. The Heathrow Express, only fifteen minutes to London, wasn't running because of mechanical problems. We waited a while for it to reopen over a hot breakfast and finally gave up and took the hour-long Tube ride to King's Cross, where we caught a train to Grantham in Lincolnshire. As soon as we arrived at beautiful Harlaxton College, where I had taught for the semester when I hatched the plan to walk Hadrian's Wall, my anxiety felt swept away. "Whilst there," as they say in England, we enjoyed seeing old friends and staying, by chance, in the stunningly beautiful Schroeder Suite, where brides and grooms usually stay. Harlaxton Manor is a restored Victorian neo-Gothic house with over 350 rooms, and we spent two nights in the nicest one, the same room my mother had stayed in for five days when she visited during my teaching semester in 2014. I was able to do one more "tune up" hike, with full pack, of about six miles along public footpaths toward Denton, around the Denton reservoir to see some birds, and back along the towpath of the Grantham-Notthingham canal to Harlaxton. I felt good and my confidence soared. Six miles—remember that number.

Anne had a conference in Gothenburg, Sweden, which was how she had paid for her flight over to Europe. I tagged along. We had never been to Sweden and while she toiled away listening to papers on health economics, I took the ferry three days in a row to the island of Vrångö. This is the southernmost inhabited island in the archipelago south of Gothenburg and the end of the line for the ferry that was included in a day pass to the city's metro system. The ferry trip itself was a beautiful ride between the islands dotted with summer homes, fishing villages, and working ports. I walked around the island looking for birds and practicing with the GoPro. There were eiders and other ducks along the way and cuckoos and nightingales on Vrångö. Even though I didn't carry my full backpack, only a satchel, I actually thought this was more practice for the hike—gentle, very short, flat walks! The real walk, and my anxiety, seemed far away, as did life at home.

We ate at a wonderful Michelin Star restaurant—the first time we had been to one—for a slightly delayed thirty-first-anniversary dinner. Eating well is one of our favorite things to do, and I love to cook. I'm not a trained or great chef, but I am creative. I have almost an hour's drive home at night from campus, and I often spend the time thinking through what we have in the fridge and creating the night's meal. I think the restaurant was cheaper than the Michelin Stars I've looked at in the US, but I must admit I never quite understood the kroner to dollar exchange rate, so maybe it cost twice as much as I thought it did. I enjoyed watching and talking to the very friendly chefs. There's a wonderful picture Anne took in which I look like I'm giving them advice, which I probably was. I can be a jerk about telling people what to do, but most chefs enjoy talking about food.

On Sunday we took a very early flight from Sweden to Gatwick Airport, south of London. Before taking off, we were desperate for coffee and breakfast, but everyone else in the café was drinking vodka and beer at 6 a.m. As soon as we landed, my anxiety was back in force; maybe I should have joined the Swedes and had some vodka. Blessedly, the Gatwick Express was running to Victoria Station, where I checked my extra suitcase in Left Luggage—the UK's baggage storage system—poles now attached to my backpack and brace firmly back on my knee, and then said goodbye to Anne for four days. I took the Tube back to King Cross Station to catch my train to Newcastle. The train was packed with partiers, including a loud foursome of Geordies, as they call people from the Newcastle area, and a group of Scots heading home from London who were absolutely certain they were the funniest group to ever drink a lot on a train. All they did was irritate me. I didn't have a seat reservation and was lucky to find a single on the first leg to York and then another seat to Newcastle next to a sketchy-looking man with torn shorts and bad eczema.

At Newcastle's Central Station, I transferred to the Metro, passing strung-out drug addicts and a heated argument at the other end of the platform while I waited for a train. I rode five stops to the Wallsend Metro Station, a long way from the city center. As the Metro rumbled east, I started worrying about the distance from my destination that night as I rode farther and farther away. I was eyeing both my fellow passengers, who were eyeing me back I was sure—though surely they are used to seeing people with backpacks on this Metro line—and the intermittent rain showers with foreboding. Great . . . rain on the first day. I had actually chosen May rather than June to experience a wider range of weather—what was I thinking? The rain was quite heavy when I alighted at Wallsend; the jocular sign with a Latin translation for "metro station"—Raedarum publicarum Statio ("public wagons station")—did little to lighten the gray concrete platform. I waited for the rain to ease up and then paid a quick visit to the visitor center at the Roman fort of Segendunum, just a block down Station Road in a brick neighborhood of cafes and offices. There was a nice museum with maps and Roman artifacts and a nine-story, space-age observation tower, hardly Roman at all. They had a locker in which to store all my gear while I went upstairs. Of course, it was hard to fit it in there, and I made a mess getting it back out when everything fell on the floor and the poles came apart. Everything I was supposed to carry for nine days was starting to feel very awkward. I walked upstairs to the room with a huge, 270-degree window for viewing. It had spectacular views of the large, excavated fort, but I was eager to get my wall passport purchased, stamped, and get my fresh legs on the way. It was already mid-afternoon, and I had a long way to go that evening. Longer than I realized.

I walked downhill past the Aldi store toward the path. I had asked the docent at Segendunum which way to turn once I got there—I imagined walking the wrong way for an hour, which I frequently do in new places. *Turn right, turn right, turn right*—I kept saying to myself down the short hill toward the River Tyne. Soon I was on the tarmac trail, going very slowly. My first mile was slow and, well, just clunky as I started to feel the full weight of the pack, which had never been quite this full. The water reservoir in my pack, with its little tube attached to my strap for drinking on the go, was actually empty, so I realized tomorrow's pack would be a couple pounds heavier once I filled the reservoir. Rain came and went; I put on and took off my jacket; I got hot and then cold. Nothing seemed to work, not even the data on my phone. I was trying to post the "reveal" selfie for my family and friends; only Anne and Ginna knew what I was doing, which was driving my mother crazy. Even though I was getting increasingly nervous about the whole venture, I tried to look confident to my online friends. I finally stopped, restarted my phone, posted two shots of me with the Hadrian's Way signs, and wobbled on.

Stunning indeed is Hadrian's Wall Path across the wild crags and moors of Northumberland and farm fields of Cumbria—some of the most picturesque scenery in northern England. But it starts east of Newcastle upon Tyne where grimy bridges, warehouses, factories, and abandoned railway abutments greet you during the first few miles on the path. On the western side of Newcastle lie the huge Dunston Coal Staithes across the River Tyne on the south bank, memorials to the famous coals of Newcastle where men loaded the ships heading to London. Soon after that you head away from the river across busy roads and along sidewalks on motorways until finally reaching schoolyards and greener suburban parks.

In the first of these gritty neighborhoods of council flats and drab housing estates east of Newcastle, just a mile or two down the trail from Segedunum, I looked up and saw a gang of youths blocking the trail. My guidebook had warned me that walkers had been hassled along here and I thought: *oh great . . . I'm going to get mugged before I even start.* I gripped my trekking poles and pressed ahead. Getting closer, I saw that they were eight to twelve years old. Well, I thought, there's still a lot of them and I'm wearing a pack—they could easily push me over and I couldn't get up, let alone run. "Good afternoon," I said, too loudly I'm sure. They nodded, stared at me, and then one asked if I had seen any policemen. Trick question. If I say no, I'm toast; they'll pin me down, take all my cash, and leave me on the ground wriggling like a beetle with my hands and feet in the air. I decided to keep my options open: "yes, about a mile back"—a lie but I thought a prudent lie. The reaction was priceless, especially for anyone who has seen young boys doing something they shouldn't. "Really? Where? How far is a mile?" They were so agitated. Turns out they had a little motorbike that they were trying to start, which is against the law on the trail, and my answer had sent them into a tizzy. But, to be honest, I quickened my pace a bit to get out of the neighborhood.

Soon thereafter, I followed the path—called Hadrian's Way in Newcastle—down a hill in an urban park to begin several miles along the River Tyne through downtown. That at least is what the guidebook told me I was doing. I ignored the ripped black plastic on the Hadrian's Way sign at the top of a hill and all the bikes taking the right fork while I went left. I probably should have been more alarmed when a fence blocked the path, but it was just covering a large hole and easy enough to go around in the woods. Down the hill I went—to discover a major construction site blocking the entire river trail. There was a tall digging machine, with a forty-foot-high tower, a tall security fence, and a sign with the words: Danger—Deep Excavations. My spirits sank again. I ended up walking— slowly and carefully!—along the steep, muddy, and slippery upper bank above the construction retaining wall, then crossing the iron fence on the river side, and walking a bit faster but just as carefully along the stone embankment until I was clear of the long site. I had started the GoPro once I turned left down toward the river, so a decent part of this adventure is in a short movie. While walking along the embankment, I said out loud (and I'm not making this up) the old Bugs Bunny refrain from the cartoon when he pops out of his hole: "I should have taken a left turn at Albuquerque!," to which I added, "or a right turn at the bike trail." As much as I had feared the gang of ten-year-old boys, falling into the River Tyne with a backpack would probably have meant drowning. But I reached the end of the construction site, tossed my pack over the iron rail, and climbed back to safety, hoping that there would be no more obstacles for the day.

Fortunately, it was just after I had passed to safety that I learned that all this digging was remediation for some chemical plant. It was still early, not quite an hour from Segendunum, and my confidence was boosted by escaping the gang of youths, making it through the construction site, reconnecting to the proper path, and, hopefully, avoiding cancerous water. I decided I wasn't contaminated as well and moved on.

I continued on the busy path through the aptly named Riverside Park, passing groups of fishermen, families grilling supper, and cyclists. There was a small parking lot to my right, and I saw the end of the path where sensible people came down to the river by following the diversion and avoiding massive holes and near-death. Leaving the park at a row of nice houses on the river, I soon came across St. Peter's Marina, opened by Her Royal Highness the Princess of Wales on April 3, 1991—a plaque proudly proclaimed. The trail then turned away from the river through some bleak parking lots before returning to the Tyne in the revitalized center of Newcastle. There was the famous series of five bridges, starting with the Millennium Bridge, not unlike the one in London that had to be closed and re-engineered when sonic vibrations made it unfit for foot traffic. I passed under it without testing its soundness since there was no reason to cross the river. The southern bank of the river was dominated by repurposed factories and mills, which I figured were now luxury flats, and the sleek glass of the modern BALTIC Center for Contemporary Art. I walked along the northern embankment, which was dotted with pubs, cafes, and restaurants on the ground floor of new office buildings. It was quiet on a Sunday evening, although the Quayside Pub, where I stopped for a pee and to refill my water bottle, had plenty of customers staring at me oddly.

As I walked through the city, I was thinking about how Rome in many ways invented modern urbanization. The words "urban" and "suburban" are Latin words, of course. Modern and Roman cities share a number of characteristics—the grand buildings of the ancient Roman Forum and the mall in Washington, DC; London squares and Italian piazzas; large religious structures, great theaters, and stadiums. And slums. Rome had dense urban buildings, *insulae*, where hundreds and thousands of *humiliores* or lower-class people lived in apartment rooms five or six stories high. An appropriate start to a walk along Hadrian's Roman Wall, I thought.

In the midst of this urban landscape—literally, in the very center of Newcastle—I saw the black-legged kittiwakes, my first "lifer" birds of the trip. (A "lifer" is a bird species that is new to you; it's the first sighting in your life.) They look somewhat like common sea gulls you might see anywhere in the US but are in fact more delicate, smaller, with a more pleasing cry. They are not scavengers but true sea birds who fish for their food, and this is their farthest inland nesting colony in the world. In the midst of all the post-industrial urban blight and decay I had walked through that afternoon into the old city of Newcastle, built on its former glory of coal, these birds appeared from nature as a symbol of hope. And all around me were new, upscale offices and flats in a city that used to send coal around the world. It was a moment to ponder, kittiwakes in Newcastle.

The kittiwakes were a bright spot in a hard first day but led me down a somewhat false path for the rest of the walk. They spoiled me: a flock of beautiful "lifer" birds in the perfect setting for juxtaposition and symbolic interpretation. And so every day henceforth I looked for "the bird of the day," without much success. There were candidates—the chaffinches and English robins, two of the most common birds in England, that I often struggled to identify; the large flock of pheasants in the field near Aydon Castle; the kestrel hovering in the wind at Blackcarts on the coldest day near the northernmost point on the wall; the curlews calling in the field near Cawfields. The noisiest candidate was the almost omnipresent Eurasian oystercatcher. Oystercatchers were everywhere across Northumberland and Cumbria, loud and aggressive when compared to our shy eastern Atlantic shorebird. But as the bird of the trek, I choose skylarks. Skylarks sing from the air along the moors and crags, in sun, rain, and mist. Skylarks' singing in the rain captures well the mood of the walk for me.

The rest of my way through Newcastle was clear. Somewhere past the Dunston Coal Staithes, the tarmac trail turned away from the River Tyne uphill into a business park and I soon found myself walking along the A695 highway for well over a mile. No motorist would ever know that this sidewalk along a busy, six-lane suburban road was Hadrian's Way unless they could see the small signs for walkers with the white oak of the UK National Trails. Eventually I crossed over the road and went up a steeper hill where the path joined a converted rail trail through suburban parks and school yards. I was finally among green grass and trees rather than warehouses, office buildings, and traffic. I had already walked nine miles that day (remember the six miles at Harlaxton that gave me so much confidence?), and I only had a mile or so left. Or so I thought.

Runners and cyclists returned to the trail as afternoon became evening. I passed an abandoned, eerie, roofless factory in the middle of the woods as dusk began to fall. As I approached Leamington, I realized my inn for the night was in Newburn, about two miles farther along. I quickened my pace considerably. Despite the earlier obstacles on the trail and the longer distance of over twelve rather than the ten miles planned, I made it to my room at the Keelman, which adjoins the blessedly welcome Big Lantern Pub and Brewery, just in time. Quickly refreshed with a pint and a shower, I ordered dinner at 8:53 before the kitchen closed at 9:00 and fell asleep early.

The next two days were smoother walking, until I came face-to-face with a bull.

CHAPTER 2

COMMON BUZZARDS

🦅 Attackers

"**H**ANDS IN THE AIR! ON THE GROUND! NOW!**" I turned and put my hands in the air and started to kneel. Eight police officers were pointing very large rifles at me about 100 feet away.

I almost didn't make it to Hadrian's Wall.

It was the day before my fifty-fifth birthday, three months before we flew to England. I had left my 11 a.m. class and began walking across campus to a faculty book group I was leading over lunch. It was a gray, sloppy day in the low 40s, a thaw after some snow. I cut through the science building, and as I was going out, a colleague asked, "Why are there so many police on campus? They're asking about Lu Hamilton." She had just seen several police, with rifles, walking into the administration building, where my office also was at the time. I stepped outside and walked past the building, feeling a bit unsettled, when a large man walked out toward me. He was wearing jeans, a black t-shirt, and a stocking cap, and had a pistol tucked in his belt. This was not a uniformed officer with a rifle. This was the shooter they were looking for.

I panicked.

He stared at me. I turned my head and walked a bit faster. At some point I veered off the path through a small patch of lawn toward the parking lot. I broke into a run. All of sudden men were screaming at me. "Police! Stop or we will shoot! Police!"

I crossed the path before turning and saw a row of rifles held by officers aiming and ready to shoot me. Two other officers with pistols were running toward me, including the one who had made me panic. I put my hands up. I thought I was dead, and I think I would have been shot in the back if I hadn't turned. "On the ground! Now!" I paused. "NOW!" I went to my knees, my hands still up. "On the ground, sir! We mean it!"

At that point I must have figured I wasn't going to be shot after all because I looked down at the muddy ground and thought, *I wore a really nice sweater today, and I don't want to get muddy.* But I went down anyway. Immediately, they were all around me. One of the men with a pistol was on me with his knee on my back.

"Where's your ID?"

"In my left pocket, my wallet," I answered. I was on the ground, book and file folder in one hand, when they read my name and let me get up.

"Lu Hamilton! Lu Hamilton! Do you know where Lu Hamilton is!?!" It was like Jason Bourne in all those movies—"Treadstone! What do you know about Treadstone!"

I squinted and said, "Maybe the gym?" I knew he was a regular player in the noon faculty/staff basketball game.

"Where is the gym, sir!"

I motioned and said, "Over that way," and most of them ran off. The police had invaded campus without a map?

By then a few colleagues were approaching. One officer, a local police lieutenant, stayed with me; maybe there was another. "Are you alright?" No, I wasn't. I was in shock, but I said I would be OK. We chatted a bit, and I walked off with my colleagues toward our lunch meeting for the book group. I was shaking and wishing I had driven myself that day rather than ride with the carpool. I couldn't leave and go home, which I would have done that very second. I went into the building, and within minutes we received a notice to shelter in place.

Unlike many of my colleagues stuck in offices or the library, we had lunch and were in a fairly good-sized group. I sat more or less silent for about an hour while people tried to take care of me. I talked to Anne and other family and messaged a friend who knew Lu. In our connected world, Ginna in North Carolina heard more about what had happened from friends texting her than those of us on the scene. Of course I posted on Facebook to let everyone know and tried to sound better than I felt: *What you look like after eight police with rifles make you lie down in the mud and put your hands out. #wabashlockdown* The photo was of me in the conference room, showing the mud on my sweater, mugging a bit with a wide open mouth to express "Wow!" It sounds so breezy now. Laugh it off as a dirty sweater.

And that evening on Facebook: *What a day. I had a weird brush with Fate/Tyche/Fortuna/Karma. I'll be fine. Wabash College had a brush with a potential major tragedy. There's a lot to learn and change to get safer—tomorrow isn't soon enough to start. And a family has been destroyed forever by someone many of us knew. Given that, I'm really fine. Thanks for all the likes and concern and please think and pray for Lu and his family.*

I wasn't OK. I don't know why I said "I'll be fine." At least I was better that evening, relieved to be home and still alive. Our parish priest came over to visit, and we had dinner with friends who had known the shooter longer than me. They were disturbed by everything, but they hadn't faced their death by police fire seven hours earlier.

Slowly, details emerged while we waited through the lockdown, while others emerged much later. A woman and child had been murdered that morning in my town of Zionsville, and Lu Hamilton had been filmed on a security camera. (The woman's husband worked in security and saw the whole thing on video after she didn't return his calls.) The police knew Lu had then come to campus, where he worked in the development office as a fundraiser. A few staff had seen him, and the police soon followed. I learned later that several different units had arrived right before I walked across campus, in addition to the local police who had started the manhunt. So the various forces—law enforcement officials from two counties, the city police, ATF, and who the hell knows who else—were not synchronized. The man who put me in a panic was apparently "undercover SWAT," which still makes no sense to me; he looked like the profile of a shooter. And I learned they gave the order to shelter in place right after my near-miss, to avoid another mistake. Damn. I could have missed all that if they had ordered the lockdown just five or ten minutes earlier.

We were on lockdown for a few hours. I eyed the window, wondering if Lu, whom I knew but not well, was going to drive by the building and start shooting. I avoided the window facing the street while others laughed and passed the time. No one was in the state I was in. Slowly, the police checked all the buildings one by one and released students and faculty. I learned that at some point they knew Hamilton left campus in a Wabash College vehicle and drove to a downtown hotel. The lockdown, which included updates by email and text, was a ruse to keep him off guard while another SWAT team moved in. He shot himself in the room after exchanging fire with the officers.

This was the closest encounter with my own death I had ever had, and I still, three years later, have visions of being shot in the back with multiple high-powered rifle bullets while running. I'm not proud of that.

The next day, my birthday, I drove down to Brown County to look for birds and try to relax in a peaceful setting. I visited our church camp, drove around Lake Lemon, and stopped at a few nature preserves. I still had to deal with fallout—a student who had witnessed my near-miss reported to the editor of a paper at DePauw University that he wasn't sure how I was involved in the murders. After several emails and a phone call with the young editor—"Why didn't you call or email me?" "We assumed you were in jail."—the story was taken down from their website.

Going back to campus on Friday was hard. I'm not sure I had to go—people would have understood if I took a day off—but I did. I jumped at every sound. I looked over my shoulder. I barely got through my lecture class, where I acknowledged but didn't discuss the events of two days earlier. I didn't have any energy to teach my freshman colloquium at 11, but we met and I talked about what had happened. I was ashamed of running but I told them I panicked. At some point that day, I talked to the dean and president and went home early. To this day, I always carry my cell phone and note men on campus who don't seem to belong; it's a small enough college that this isn't too hard.

Somehow I managed to get an appointment with the therapist that afternoon who had worked with our son as well as Anne and me from time to time. I told her about the shame I felt, the deep shame of running away. When she learned I had shared the details of panicking with my freshmen, she told me I could have taught a class on the cognitive therapy she was suggesting. She said it was a classic, textbook way to get over shame: to confess it, to own it, and to move on.

What does it take to share failure? To open up to our shame? Would this have helped my father? We are all ashamed of something, maybe many things, but we all handle it differently. There should be no shame in depression, but there clearly was for my father. My father's professional life was a factor—maybe the factor—that led him to put the hose in the car that afternoon in our driveway. And my brush with the police that day was but one dramatic episode in a professional life that has been quite complicated at times.

Three weeks after I was taken down by the police, I learned that my nemesis at work had put a pistol in his mouth and pulled the trigger.

Let's back up a bit for that story—twenty-five years.

The week after my father died, the four surviving children—me, my older sister, Beth, and younger sisters, Sarah and Patsy—met in our red library room, called the Study, with my father's therapist, a man he had known well before becoming so ill. My parents had started therapy with him while I was in college perhaps ten years earlier; I think it was spurred on by my mother enrolling in graduate school at Candler Theological School and eventually starting a new vocational path as a hospital chaplain at Grady Hospital. I remember considerable conflict one spring break from college, an outright fight and tears (Was I crying? My mother? I can't recall.)—a scene played out in thousands of households in the '70s and '80s as women started new careers and ventures that upset the routines of husbands who judged their marriages and family lives by the standards of the 1950s, when they were first married. The therapist also attended their church, St. Anne's Episcopal Church, which had been my church as well through high school and where my father's funeral had been held a few days earlier.

That morning in the Study, he asked us all to say what we had learned from this experience. I answered: "Bend, don't break. Bend, don't break." That became a core lesson for me. No matter how bad it seems, no matter what you've done or what you think you've done, it's not worth breaking apart. Bend, don't break.

This life lesson was crucial, unfortunately, many times in my professional life, and not just the week after the lockdown. Small liberal arts colleges are notoriously difficult places socially and politically, but my department was deeply divided and often dysfunctional. Religion has a hold on many people in their life, of course. The college is officially secular and has never been church-affiliated, but the department had long operated as a sort of Christian base for the college and students.

The chair who hired me was Bill Placher, now deceased, a theologian and professor of philosophy and religion. He was a beloved teacher by generations of students and remains a highly respected theologian in church and academic circles for his crystal-clear writing on complex subjects. Bill was an active preacher in his Presbyterian Church as well as in the small chapel that had been built adjacent to the religion department for Christian services when the main college chapel service veered secular, as happened at almost all small colleges in the 1960s.

My nemesis, in contrast, was exactly my age but had gone through graduate school much faster than me and had been there for years when I was hired. Will was considered both brilliant and very difficult to get along with by colleagues. He, too, was an active Christian theologian, very close to many students, and a strong proponent of sharing his faith in the classroom. I represented a more critical approach to the teaching of religion, actually called historical-critical studies in biblical studies. While my view remains far and away the dominant approach in departments across the country and western world, Will's was a strong voice against me. The disagreement over faith and teaching in the liberal arts has even made it into his books and an article he wrote with Bill, in which they had a dialogue about teaching and faith perspectives.

But the disagreements over teaching soon became personal and nasty. A year after I was hired, Will started a pattern of harassing me that continued for years. He yelled at me one Friday afternoon early in my second year for over an hour, leading to the first of many distraught weekends: anxious all night, waking up early, bad dreams, a pit of despair in my gut. Anne could have stayed at Stanford longer, and neither of us was very happy about this small college and small Indiana town so far. We were going to Ann Arbor to see family that weekend, and I went over to Bill's house on Sunday night to talk it over. Bill promised intervention, but that never worked.

Will's behavior got worse and worse. He had been given free rein to argue with and attack and harass people on campus for over twenty years. Behavior that would have someone fired today was tolerated in the last century, as we've learned from the many public figures recently exposed for harassment that often goes back for decades. They were used to him, and in discussions with senior faculty, I would often hear, "That's just how he is," or stories about how they too were at the receiving end of scathing emails. They remembered him as a brilliant student back a few decades, which I did not. In other words, his bullying behavior was tolerated, which, as my friend and comedian Brad Tassell has written about, is how you feed a bully.

I hated him. For years I avoided him in the halls or as we crossed campus. I despised everything about him: his beliefs, actions, and cruelty; his hypocrisy about religion, in my mind. This guy opposed me at every review, going so far as soliciting students against me by "poisoning the well" and leaking comments from my file to student publications. He dominated my professional life and much of our home life for the next five years. Some colleagues in other departments knew about this, but many thought it was a "Bob problem," that I aggravated him, rather than the harassing and deeply unprofessional behavior that it was. Nobody knew what to do about it, especially me. Will was already tenured and was even promoted during this period. He was invited to give a prestigious campus lecture. I wanted to bend and not break, but I had to fight for my career, which included applying and interviewing elsewhere, which I was afraid would be considered disloyal and undercut my chances of tenure. So I had to keep that quiet.

And I won, sort of, receiving tenure and two highly prestigious research fellowships that got me back to Stanford for another year and an additional semester of research leave. For the first time since Will attacked me that September afternoon, I felt free.

While I was at Stanford, he went on to attack female colleagues for being feminists, often to students in his classes. He advised the radically conservative, "traditional" student magazine, which was not run or supported by the college but by a private foundation. The magazine regularly pushed to the edge of slander with its back-page parodies of faculty members. Many of my colleagues received this treatment and saw it as a perverse badge of honor. During that fourth-year review, when Will leaked comments to the students, they parodied me with a photo of me in my office and a target on my head with the joke that Islamic groups had issued a death-threat against me for challenging students' beliefs. Religious belief was central to our conflict since Will had become more and more religiously as well as politically conservative and even converted to Roman Catholicism. But there must have been deeper mental problems.

During my tenure review, the department gave Will equal time in the final letter to the personnel committee, the deans who made the recommendation for tenure to the president. The vote in the department was 3-1, but the letter made it sound like it had been 50-50. When one of the associate deans came to our house with a bottle of champagne to celebrate my tenure, she said to Anne, "They gave him a copy of *that* letter?" A friend once told me to choose my enemies wisely. Will had lost all influence beyond maybe two or three faculty members.

But his erratic behavior continued, no longer always against me. Having won a permanent position on the faculty, I began to face up to him more strongly and show some fight. Generally, it was easier to avoid him and other controversies in the department. Bend, don't break.

Then our new dean began to build a file of his abusive behavior against me, female faculty, and even students. There are too many stories to tell, and many of them are not my stories. There was another Friday afternoon "abuse session," disguised as a departmental meeting but really a trap, when he harassed me for well over an hour about a research grant I had received and all the ways I was out of line. But he finally had to leave, which is very difficult to do when you're a tenured professor. Colleges do not take this step lightly, although I believe he was "allowed to resign." But he must have crossed some line that even a senior faculty member cannot cross.

I had no idea this had happened until someone told me in August at a pre-semester meeting. I was standing in the buffet line for our lunch, and I could not believe what I was hearing. A retired faculty colleague, who had been an associate dean on my tenure review, compared this to a cancer being removed from campus. A student who had graduated a few years before told me he had a dread of running into this guy in Indianapolis at some event. I felt free again after a thirteen-year burden of personal and professional abuse. Anne and I celebrated for months.

But it turned out to be false freedom. A month after I was surrounded by police rifles, and two months before I started walking Hadrian's Wall, I found out Will had committed suicide. We were visiting our daughter in North Carolina during my spring break. I was in a coffee shop, having just met someone with whom to discuss some religion projects when I got the call. For anyone who has experienced a family suicide, this is hard news. My father's first botched attempt was with a rifle. I celebrated this man's removal from my professional life but would never want this to happen to any family—ever.

A coda to this story is that while Will had converted to Catholicism, the service was held in the Disciples of Christ Church that he had grown up in. I did not attend the funeral.

A year later, I moved my administrative home to the history department, relieving another source of tension. Bend, don't break.

I think about this a lot as I approach the age when my father killed himself because it could have been his professional life that killed him. My father was a lawyer and, when I was a child, "the Firm" was an all-encompassing, beneficent presence for our family. There were summer swimming parties at the small lake owned by one of the senior partners and a Christmas party every year with Santa Claus—a big deal because we got extra presents. And there was shrimp, which I still adore. Once I was eating a lot of shrimp at the buffet when an unknown woman said that if I ate too much shrimp I would turn into one. "He already is!" said her teenage daughter. I was about eight years old.

My parents' social life involved the law firm as well as church friends. My memory of my younger years was of large parties downstairs in our house with bright chatter and laughter. I would sit at the top of the stairs, listen, and smell the perfume and cigarette smoke of the late 1960s and early 1970s. After a while cigarettes were banned from the house and dinner parties replaced cocktail parties as my mother learned more and more about "gourmet cooking," as it was called in the '70s, well before the foodie revolutions that followed. She has always been, and remains, an excellent cook, but I put this in scare quotes because there was a *New Yorker* cartoon on the bulletin board in our breakfast room, showing a disheveled woman surrounded by dirty pots and pans and her husband with a guest saying, "Gladys is a gourmet cook, aren't you dear?" The older children were pressed into service for these dinner parties, washing dishes and sometimes even serving. (Never eating, however; we ate earlier, something fast and probably cheap.)

In the early '70s, my parents became disciples of Adele Davis and her books about healthy eating. White bread and sugared cereals were banished from the house and replaced by steak and eggs; brown bread; a raft of vitamins every morning on a small Chinese spice bowl, color-coded for each child; along with the most revolting brewer's yeast protein drinks ever concocted by humankind called Pep-Up. We—my brother and I in particular—tried to flush it down the toilet but eventually accepted our fate. I remember hiding some food that was particularly healthy under my chair one night, probably eggplant and lentils—something I would seek out today. For Christmas, my brother would get a loaf of white bread. We had strict limits on cokes and candy as well, which wasn't all bad since one time, at a children's party for the law firm, I ate ten doughnuts and broke out in hives the next day.

Health and exercise were central to my father's life. He rode his bicycle to the corner store or over to the tennis courts at the club we belonged to, which we had to do as well, to my great chagrin, while my friends and classmates at the pool were being dropped off and picked up. My mother was famously carpool-averse, dropping friends and neighbors in my carpools off at the top of a street, with over a quarter-mile walk left, rather than drive down the street and back. My father opened a branch office of the law firm near our house, the first on the north side of Atlanta rather than downtown, and was able to ride his bike to work. Eventually, these exercise patterns took with me as well.

Sometime in the year before he died, before our summer at the farm, he was named in a malpractice suit. The client put my father's name in along with anyone remotely associated with the matter at the law firm. That's about all I learned from my mother.

He wasn't responsible. I'll take that as the truth, though I never investigated further and I don't want to because it would be too painful. Perhaps this was a convenient story. I only learned this story about the lawsuit after he died or during the last few months when he was seriously depressed and no longer going to the office. It hit at his core and he began to slowly sink into depression. He couldn't bend and he eventually broke.

By March, when we visited Atlanta during Yale's two-week spring recess, it was clear that my father was in very bad shape. The depression had a serious grip on him. He had even taken a leave of absence at work and told the law firm that the doctor was worried about his heart. He was as fit as any man in his late fifties could be when he got depression, so the fib was patently obvious. And yet he did have a broken heart, the metaphorical type of heart. He had converted to Catholicism years before, but during these months returned to St. Anne's Episcopal Church. This was where his funeral would be held two months later.

His profession was at the center of his identity, as it was for so many men of his generation, as well as mine. We are what we do. One of the worst periods in my life was a few years before my father killed himself when I had to decide whether to pursue a one-year master's degree or accept the offer from Yale for a Ph.D. with only partial funding. Should I roll the dice and hope for more money the following year? This would decide my career—my identity. I remember heaving over, sick to my stomach in our little office room that would become a nursery for our son a few years later, shaking with anxiety and tension over the decision.

My father was in a much different place back then, only two years before his depression. He was able to reach out and connect emotionally. He had progressed in therapy, developed a spiritual, Jungian outlook on life, and was working through issues around the death of my brother. He no longer seemed as tense as the man I grew up around. A few years before he died, our first dog, Molly, died suddenly on her first birthday. She went quickly from cardiomyopathy, the enlarged heart that every now and then fells a teenager or young athlete. He was very understanding on the phone and helped me get in touch with my sudden, surprising grief. Our foreheads were sore from crying—this was our first child! And he cried on the phone too. At the time I thought this was the "new Dad" that would last for years. Looking back, I see now that it was his peak. But we don't see our highest point until much later, after we decline.

The decision in that office in April to get a Ph.D. led eventually to the twelve years fighting with my nemesis. I have never been depressed about all the abuse and tension in my professional life, only angry, anxious, or frustrated. Often it engaged my "fight or flight" instincts. Sometimes it pushed me to think harder about ways to "make my own shop" within the department. Rather than depression, I've had bouts of extreme anxiety, due to personal rather than professional reasons, such as when our son was having a very tough time out of college.

I am sure my father's depression was deeply personal as well, but there's so much I don't know about why. He was ambitious and highly disciplined almost his entire life, but the dark side of those traits was he could be rigid and unable to handle failure. Was there something in his childhood that we didn't know about? I didn't know his father very well because he died when I was young, but his mother was a warm, delightful lady whom we named our daughter after. But of course families keep secrets. My mother told some story about a very strict caregiver, but it was kind of vague. Was it genetic? Probably all of this and more. It could have been everything—I don't think it was just one thing, even if the malpractice suit was the main trigger.

I've learned to keep my work and social life fairly separate. I think I work well with most people on campus, and I do a good job. And then I go home about an hour away to a different social circle. We have made a nice home here after ten years and we enjoy our friends in the "Village," as we call it, the quirky old downtown area of the town. It became oppressive to work intensely with people and then spend almost all your social life with the same people, and now we enjoy the distance. I have a good friend in Atlanta, a lawyer in a different firm from my father, who has indicated from time to time that socializing within a law firm has the same oppressiveness as the social life of a small college in a small town.

I don't know who my father's friends were when he died. I'm sure some of these people were from the law firm but I don't know if they were good friends. In the '70s and '80s there were church friends and tennis friends. But then he changed churches. In later years, the last ten years of his life of so, he spent more time with clients, I think, and less with partners at the office. My parents entertained them often and even stayed with different clients who had become friends in New York or England. But I don't think there was anyone to talk to in the last year or two. At least, I didn't know about anyone. I think about that as I approach fifty-eight.

Fortunately, my professional story is much happier now than a few years ago and clearly in a far better place than my father's was as he approached fifty-eight. And my profession is my identity. But I carried a lot inside my head as well as on my back on my walk across England. In April, about a month before the walk along Hadrian's Wall and the same day I hurt my right knee so badly, I received word of a decision at work that was one of the worst professional moments of my career. The progress I had made in the previous four years since my nemesis left seemed finished and my career essentially at an end. On the walk a month later, I was still fuming.

CHAPTER 3

PHEASANTS

~ Gamebirds

I woke up early with the sun on that second day in the Keelman, a downside of the long May days in England when the sun rises before 5:00 a.m. But I snoozed on and off until 8:00 or so and, after a shower to ease some of the stiffness from my first day's walk across the cityscape of Newcastle, wandered over to the restaurant sunroom for a huge English breakfast on a fine morning. I was wearing sandals; my feet were already sore, and I felt early pains that would grow significantly over the next eight days. But I was happy, contented even, in the fine English sunshine. I had finished day 1! It was a lot harder than expected, but today would be easier, with an earlier start and not too long a hike. Or so I thought.

I got in a brief discussion at breakfast with an American couple heading the other direction. We chatted about their day ahead. I warned them: "Watch out in River Park! There's a diversion in the path." But they exhibited the confidence of people with long days already behind them and no fear of the hike on tarmac ahead. They did ask me if I was hiking in those sandals, however, which does suggest something about either their air of superiority or how inept I must have looked to them as a walker. I assured them I had left my boots in the room and turned to conversation, after they left, with a much politer English gentleman about his many rambles along the wall path.

It took a while to get packed up, and I had to pay for my room and meal in the bar of the Big Lantern Pub, where I waited for what seemed like an hour behind three English women ordering enormously complicated cold drinks from the one man working there. I strolled off mid-morning in suburban parkland along the River Tyne, passing grannies with prams and passed by morning runners. I felt great listening to the birds in the reeds by the river.

Soon I was in the woodlands, where Hadrian's Wall Way becomes Hadrian's Wall Path, the name that lasts to the end of the trail in Bowness-on-Solway. The path leaves the River Tyne for good at Close House Golf Course, where the route shows signs of an uneasy truce between National Trail planners and golf resort executives. The path winds through the grounds in an obvious attempt to keep hikers completely hidden from golfers by cutting through woods and behind sheds and hedgerows as if the sight of backpacks and walking sticks would precipitate triple-putts. Perhaps, like the farmers and the cowboys in Oklahoma, golfers and walkers are not friends, but no one took notice of me—I was well-hidden, of course. Soon I was walking up a steep hill out of the river valley with sumptuous views of bright yellow rapeseed fields to the village of Heddon-on-Wall, where indeed I saw my first piece of actual wall since Segendunum.

There's not much wall left along the walk, maybe 15 out of the 84 miles of trail. It took me the long Sunday and almost two hours that morning—an hour and forty-eight minutes and 2.26 miles to be precise, thanks to the phone app I carried on the route—to find this long bit of wall. What is excavated only suggests the ancient wall. The original plan of Hadrian's Wall was very regular, although there's a lot of evidence that the Romans made some things up as they went along or had to change the plan. Heddon-on-Wall has the longest stretch of broad wall—wall the size of its broad foundations—still around today. But by the middle of the wall, the Roman legions had abandoned this breadth and started building narrow wall on top of the broad foundations. Signs of changes along the way include Turret 29A, which would have been the first turret, moving east to west, between Roman miles 29 and 30 of the wall. The Roman legions built the turret before the wall caught up with them, it appears, because they built two pieces of pre-wall, which sticks out like small wings on either side of the turret, to connect to the broad wall when it arrived from the east. But what came along and passed on to the west was narrow wall, so the plans had changed by the time they got to Black Carts, the northernmost stretch of wall. Farther west, walkers can see excavated narrow wall with the original, broader foundations near the village of Gilsland, right at the border of the two English counties of Northumberland and Cumbria.

The wall ran from large fort to large fort across the narrowest part of what was then Britannia, starting at the River Tyne in the east and finishing at the Firth of Solway in the west (in the U.S., we might call it Solway Bay). The western half was originally built out of turf rather than stone, and there are still hilly remnants of the turf wall west of Birdoswald Roman Fort, the last excavated fort on the western side of Cumbria. Every Roman mile there was a milecastle, a small fort or "fortlet" in wall parlance, and in between each milecastle were two turrets. But that's hard to see today. Rather than a fortlet every mile and two towers between, there are ruins of the milecastles and turrets here and there, or sometimes just the shape of one outlined in the crops. Even the great Roman forts are often just big lumpy squares in a field, unexcavated or excavated and filled again.

We're not even sure how high the wall was or whether there was a walk and parapet along the top, although most scholars think there was. Arguing about the height and parapet seems to be the chief pastime of wall archaeologists; I have one scholarly book summarizing just about every theory and fact about the wall and its history. I don't recommend this book unless you like a nice nap in the afternoon. Anyway, a parapet and walk certainly fits with my imagination of the original wall. I get this from the movies, where Roman soldiers with large, curved shields and spears pace along the wall behind these had-to-be-there parapets, looking for barbarians while mumbling to each other in lower-class British accents. Luckily for my imagination, there's evidence engraved on the Rudge Cup, a ceremonial dish that might have functioned as an ancient Roman version of the gold watch given to a retiree. It's inscribed with the names of five forts at the western end of Hadrian's Wall and a picture that suggests a regular wall with large rectangular panes. The schematic drawing shows towers, perhaps the forts, with parapets where my East London Roman soldiers could pace. The British Museum has a replica of the cup, but the real one is the property of the Duke of Northumberland and resides in Alnwick Castle, whose noble courtyard appears in both the Harry Potter films and the final season of *Downton Abbey*.

Where there is no wall, there are often magnificent earthworks. As stunning as the remains of the wall itself are today in the fields and farmlands of northern England, the ditch on its north side and vallum along the south side are almost equally impressive today. The ditch is just that—a steep "V" along the north of the wall, still visible along many miles of the path. You can imagine it would have been very hard to charge a wall, however high it might have been, with this ditch in the way. In the middle of England and hence the middle of the wall, there are steep crags along a ridge called the Whin Sill. Staring over these steep cliffs to the north, it's very clear why the Romans didn't need a ditch along here. (Later we'll fantasize about pushing someone off the crags). And at the wall's northernmost point, Limestone Corner near Black Carts Farm, the Roman engineers gave up trying to dig the northern ditch in the basalt whinstone, which we can see in huge blocks of the stone still lying on the ground north of the wall.

The purpose of the vallum on the south side is less clear. It was a huge, flat ditch, twenty feet wide and ten feet deep, with two large berms on either side. Since it follows the lines of some later forts on the south side of the wall, it was probably built later than the wall and might have marked a military zone. The Romans cut roads into the vallum later, however, and built forts on top of it. To think that these massive Roman earthworks have survived almost two thousand years of farming, grazing, and even quarrying is nothing short of impressive. Walking in and along the ditch and vallum, you get a sense of the size and scope of the construction since the wall itself comes and goes in short bits.

Hadrian became Emperor of Rome in 117 CE under somewhat dicey circumstances when the Emperor Trajan died. Trajan was Hadrian's guardian and apparently planned to make Hadrian emperor, but never got around to publicly declaring the succession. Perhaps he was ambivalent; his final years were marked by heavy drinking and failed campaigns against Parthia, an ancient part of Mesopotamia that today is roughly northern Iraq and Iran. Hadrian and Trajan's wife, Plotina, a supporter of Hadrian's his entire life, had to scramble to make his accession look legitimate in Rome, even though he had the support of the army all along. This could be why the often forward-thinking Hadrian made sure both his successor, Antoninus Pius, and his successor's successor, Marcus Aurelius (the one who shows up in the film *Gladiator*), were chosen before he died.

Hadrian reigned from 117–138, after Trajan, and before Antoninus Pius and Marcus Aurelius. These are four of the five traditional "good emperors." These four, along with Nerva, ruled during the height of peace and prosperity in the Roman Empire, the *Pax Romana*, from the end of the first to the end of the second century. They chose their successors by adoption rather than birth, although they were all senatorial families. But, as anyone who has studied history knows, "good" is quite a relative term, depending on who's doing the labeling. Hadrian is known for his love of Greek culture and magnificent buildings, such as the Pantheon in Rome and the Temple of Zeus Olympios in Athens. He was the first emperor to sport a beard, which set a fashion for a century. But at the end of his life, he fought a bitter war against the Jews, destroying Jerusalem and renaming it Aelia Capitolina after his family and the chief Roman gods of the capitol. It was in fact Machiavelli who coined the term "good emperors" in 1503.

The wall was part of a larger plan for Hadrian. One of his early policies was to stop Trajan's military expansions in Parthia, beyond the Tigris River, and Dacia (roughly Romania today), site of bloody campaigns and one of Trajan's greatest military triumphs. The empire erupted, from Britain to Egypt to Mesopotamia, at the death of Trajan. Hadrian had to act quickly to staunch the flow of blood while also securing his own shaky succession. He made strategic retreats, negotiated treaties, and bribed kings on the borders. In other words, he began his reign by shrinking the borders of the Roman Empire, which was not popular. There was a possible assassination attempt on Hadrian during his first year as emperor, followed by the assassination of four ex-consuls by senate vote, carried out by Hadrian's man in Rome. He also spent lavishly during his first year in Rome to bribe the city back to his side. He was by no means a peaceful emperor—and he was devoted to the army—but he did not start new campaigns of expansion. A revolt against Rome in the north of Britain, which occurred during almost every new emperor's reign, probably drew his attention and perhaps started him thinking about fortified boundaries, since Britannia was on his first tour as emperor.

Before he left Rome for the first time as emperor, three years into his reign, Hadrian redrew the sacred boundary of Rome during the annual foundation ceremony of the city. Trajan had extended the empire into Dacia and Parthia but not the city's sacred boundaries; Hadrian emphatically re-drew the boundaries after giving up these very territories. This was in a sense his first wall, and the boundaries of the city were set with new boundary stones. He proceeded north to the German provinces and ordered the construction of a wooden palisade along the frontier. This palisade was clearly more a symbolic boundary than a military fortification, and it kept the soldiers busy as well. Hadrian wanted to mark the borders clearly for both the Romans and the German barbarians. His policy to not expand the empire led him to form symbolic boundaries as well as physical lines in Germania, North Africa, and Britannia.

Hadrian arrived in Britain from Germany in 122—hence the bus that runs along the wall during the summer is called the AD122. Hadrian likely surveyed a good part of the wall as well, perhaps to the high peaks of the Pennines in the center of England today where the Pennine Way crosses Hadrian's Wall Path. Hadrian was famously attracted to climbing peaks. Three legions, comprised of Roman citizens and including many engineers and skilled workers, built the wall and then returned to bases and forts in the south of Britannia. Auxiliaries, non-citizen troops from conquered provinces, manned the wall. This meant soldiers from all over, even Syria, ended up in northern England with the worst weather of the empire. I wanted to walk the wall in May when I would experience some of that weather, but I'd rather spend the winter in southern Italy, France, or Spain—the Roman heartlands.

Hadrian deserves the credit for building what we call today Hadrian's Wall, although it was called the Severan Wall until 1839 when a local clergyman, the Rev. John Hodgson, proved it had been built originally by Hadrian. Emperor Septimius Severus made significant repairs and changes to Hadrian's Wall in the third century. But it is Hadrian's Wall or the Wall of Aelius in Roman times, after Hadrian's family name. One irony is that Severus was the first "bad" emperor after the five good emperors I mentioned earlier, and his reign presaged the crises of the third century in Rome.

I stopped for tea in Heddon-on-Wall at the top of the steep hill and chatted with a fellow named Stan and his girlfriend. Stan wondered why so many Americans walked the wall path, although I met many Brits and several Germans and Dutch walkers as well. Stan had biked a good bit of the wall, and by "biked" I'm pretty sure he meant motorcycle. He seemed to warm to me when I mentioned that I had eaten last night at the Big Lamp Brewery, whose fine ales Stan was quite familiar with, and quizzed me about the TV show *American Pickers*, which I have still never seen. I then walked to view the long stretch of broad wall, which was just off the trail at the end of the village. I returned to the path and continued west along the B6318, the Military Road. This straight-as-an-arrow highway was built in 1746 by General George Wade when the English were fighting Bonnie Prince Charlie and his Scottish army. It follows the wall and, unfortunately, covers a lot of it. General Wade was in a hurry when he built the road since communication for his forces was so poor at the time. But where the wall has been covered, the ditch and vallum stand out even more.

I soon regretted my tea and started the first of many searches over the next week for a place to pee hidden from road and trail. (Someone should produce a map of discrete locations for hikers). I saw a stretch of unexcavated wall along a farm field and the now-filled-in Rudchester Fort, called Vindobala by the Romans, as clouds gathered in the west. Soon it was raining as I walked in some of the steepest ditch on the trail, according to my guidebook. But the weather was warm enough that this didn't bother me at all; I had wanted a full range of weather along the way. The rain continued as I passed between the Great Northern Lake and the Great Southern Lake of the Whittledene Reservoir. The lakes were not particularly great, in terms of size, although they pump twenty-five million gallons a day to the nearby treatment works. I was looking forward to birdwatching here, but the rain dampened my enthusiasm and there were only a few gulls and terns. I arrived at the Robin Hood Inn for a very late lunch and dried out over a pint and a cheddar-and-chutney sandwich. I sat for a while, which allowed me to see a burly fellow with a large bushy beard wearing a pink ballerina's tutu arrive at the inn. Turned out he was running the wall in four days for charity, breast cancer I think, and this was the end of his first day after running about 25 miles.

I stamped my passport for the second time on the way out and walked out into a sunny, drier afternoon, heading west at an easy pace through Wallhouses, along undulating hills with plenty of ditch and vallum but no wall. I passed Halton Red House, which was constructed from wall stones, and turned off the wall path at Halton Chesters for a planned diversion to Corbridge Roman Town south of the wall. Clouds had returned and it was completely overcast but felt dry. A road led straight south through a lumpy field, a large square that barely suggested the remains of the Roman fort called Onnum, to Halton Castle. The field was full of the wooliest, dirtiest sheep I have ever seen. There was poop everywhere, including all around the production end of the sheep. I'm glad I didn't have to shear these sheep, but perhaps they get a bath first. They looked otherwise like regular sheep with black noses, but on the other side of Halton Castle, which was a small pleasant manor-house-cum-working-farm with a single square tower, there were boutique sheep, with bushy brown wool, a white stripe on the face, and white socks on their black legs. They also had more favorable and apparently cleaner grazing land around the castle and house itself. I'd like to call them "Braveheart sheep" but the rest of their face isn't blue. When I returned home, I sent a picture to a friend who raises sheep and she replied excitedly by email, "Zwartbles!" They came from the Netherlands; their apparently practical name in Dutch means "black with a white blaze," according to the "British Wool" website.

The road behind Halton Castle headed downhill toward Corbridge, the bridge over the Cor Burn near the River Tyne. (The British also name their places very practically.) I followed the signs to Aydon Castle and soon arrived at this English heritage site—which was a mistake; I was not supposed to go to Aydon Castle at all, but rather should have turned left a mile or two back, up the steep hill of the creek valley. It was almost 5 p.m., and I had already walked over fourteen miles that day. The increasing clouds had already dampened my bright mood from the morning and now, here I was, literally at a dead end in the road.

We go along, bright and zippy, and *bam*—the road ends. Everything suddenly felt heavier: my pack, my legs, my worries. I had been certain I would become chair, finally, after years without my nemesis around. I was the senior member of the department. I had spearheaded events with students. I had set forth a vision of how we could engage the rest of the faculty who generally have no idea what we do aside from church services. I put together a group of faculty from other departments to read Lord Rabbi Jonathan Sacks's book *Not in God's Name* and talk about how to address religious conflict—this was the discussion group I was walking to when I ran from the police. But like Aydon Lane, the department was a dead end. They rejected my vision. They rejected me. There was nowhere left to go there.

The best evidence of my down state of mind facing several dead ends is that I didn't take any pictures, not even selfies showing my distress, at Aydon Castle. It was a low moment. I turned on phone data and started to look for a route on Google Maps when a couple drove up and parked by the castle to walk their dog. They kindly directed me back along another way that would connect, eventually, to the highway that led down into Corbridge. I started down this little lane, into the woods, hoping they were right. Just after crossing Cor Burn, the lane passed into fields and opened up. I could see the way forward now, and I took the only picture that afternoon—of the road ahead. I could see how I would walk to Corbridge, and I was sure that somehow I would see a way forward back on campus. Bend, don't break. It couldn't be worse than lying on the ground in the mud while SWAT teams surround you. I will think of something, but it took another year to figure out.

I walked about four miles. Even the birds came back as I passed through fields with scores of pheasants to the B6321, or Aydon Road, which crossed the busy A90 bypass. It was now hardly bucolic as I had left behind the sheep and pheasant fields. Lorries and cars passed me at alarming rates, with all the noise of narrow English highways. But at least it was the right way to dinner and a bed. And it was downhill now. The weather turned cooler and gray but stayed dry as I walked down to the town, still on the B6321, soon Main Street instead of Aydon Road. My inn was on this street, the Angel of Corbridge, a nice complement to the two angels who put me back on the right path at Aydon Castle. I checked in to my room, which was the size of a monk's cell, showered and washed clothes before enjoying a pint and a hefty burger with fried onions and a basket of chips in the Angel's restaurant.

I slept well in my small cell and woke up with the first blisters of the walk.

During Hadrian's time, Christians began to construct their own walls, the walls of orthodoxy and heresy. *We are on this side*, the Orthodox claimed; *you are on that side. You are on that side because of what you think, what you believe, and what you don't believe. And what you think changes who you are.* For Orthodox Christians, heretics were under the dominion of Satan, and heresy led to damnation.

The foundation of this wall, the demonized difference we call "heresy" today, was being built for over a hundred years before Hadrian's Wall. That story is the focus of my academic book *The Origin of Heresy*. What changes soon after Hadrian's reign is that one of the first major proponents of "orthodox" Christianity's superiority to heresy, Justin Martyr, makes a political argument as well. In his *Apology*, or defense of Christians written to Hadrian's successor Antoninus Pius, he claims that not only is his group of "right thinking" Christians the only proper type of Christians, but that they are also proper Romans, while the heretics who claim the name of Christian are not. They are really demonic. Justin's wall of heresy, in other words, dovetails with Hadrian's Wall. We Orthodox Christians are on this side with you Romans, while heretics are on the other side with the barbarians.

Hadrian certainly knew about Christians. He could have been aware of the letters about Christians between Pliny the Younger and Trajan from ten or fifteen years earlier. Pliny, governor of the Roman province along the Black Sea called Bithynia, had heard about trials of Christians but wasn't sure what to do with the ones he captured. A few he killed because of their refusal to answer questions, a typical Roman approach, but others were Roman citizens who deserved a trial. Trajan replied that Christians should not be sought out or arrested on anonymous charges, almost an ancient "don't ask, don't tell" policy. While traveling in Germany or Britain, Hadrian received a similar letter from another governor of Asia Minor, what we call western Turkey today. His reply, following Trajan, basically "leave them alone unless they cause trouble," was quoted and expanded on with some creative license by our friend Justin as part of his campaign to present his Orthodox Christian party as good Romans and all other Christians, such as Gnostics, as heretics.

There are many gods along Hadrian's Wall: Jupiter, Mars, Mercury; Fortuna, Disciplina, the goddess of Roma and the Genius of the Emperor, worshiped by soldiers and Romans in the eastern provinces; local gods such as Coventina or Faunus; and gods who traveled with the army such as the Syrian Mother Goddess and the Germanic Loki. Roman soldiers from around the empire brought their gods with them. There were at least three mithaeums in the forts along the wall—underground temples to the Persian god Mithras where bulls were sacrificed and eaten in a men-only military cult. But no churches, not for a while at least. Christianity in Britain emerged slowly, well after Hadrian's visit in 122. It was the far edge of the empire and always a bit more barbarian than nicer places such as the very Roman province in southern France, which we still call Provence. There were likely Christians in Britain by the third century, when the emperors started killing more Christians such as Saint Alban in a series of persecutions, and British bishops attended one of the first church councils called by the first Christian emperor, Constantine, in Arles, today part of Provence. But Christianity fit more easily into the relatively peaceful, Romanized south of Britain than the wilds of the north country. A few crosses and possible baptismal fonts have been found in forts along Hadrian's Wall. The God of the Christians looked over at least some if not most of the last Roman soldiers along the wall before the Romans left Britain as the empire began to collapse in 410.

Hadrian's Wall is longer than eighty-four miles. It travels across the Roman Empire and all the way to our present lives. Heresy, the Christian wall that follows Hadrian's, was an innovative, profoundly divisive, and deeply dualistic way of dealing with difference. It became foundational to Christianity, from burning heretics at the stake in the Middle Ages to the rise of the Evangelical Religious Right. The wall that early Christians built, the wall of heresy, divides us to this day. Even more fundamental and important are the effects on our politics, whether a person or group has religious affiliations and traditions or not. Political polarization has increased significantly since the 1990s (and measurably, according to some things I've read, but I am not a political scientist). The tenor of campaigns and political rhetoric echoes the heresiologists of the early Christian era. Name-calling, demonization of the other, exclusivity—these are the hallmarks of heresy.

As far as I know, Hadrian did not claim he would build a wall and the Britons would pay for it. I used this joke during and after the presidential campaign of 2016, and it was funny for a while. By the end of the Trump administration, after all the lies, gratuitous cruelty, corruption, Russian collusion, and the post-election "big lie" leading to the insurrection of 6 January, 2021, nothing about this President was funny anymore. Of course he wanted to build a wall; it's what autocrats and emperors do, but not presidents. There's still some wall standing between the US and Mexico, a remnant of the forty-fifth presidential administration, standing like Hadrian's German border of wooden stakes, a symbol of "us" and "them."

I've never been to China to see the Great Wall, but I was in Berlin in 1983, the summer I started my year abroad after college, when crossing the Berlin Wall was a major endeavor for a westerner. Crossing into and out of East Berlin was probably the tensest international moment of my first twenty-two years—actually ever. I was in Berlin for a sort of church conference focusing on international reconciliation at a church educational center. I was the only young person with a group of American grownups who had come over with their Episcopal priests, while I had been overseas already for three months, volunteering at Coventry Cathedral in England. Coventry was the headquarters of this reconciliation movement called the Community of the Cross of Nails, named from a cross of nails found in the bombed-out original cathedral after it had been "coventrated" (a neologism of the day) by the German Luftwaffe over two days in November 1941. We went to East Berlin on a Sunday to join a Christian, probably Lutheran, group on the other side for a service and meal. I recall lunch on a boat cruise. I must have put myself into some sort of unofficial helping role—the student assistant— because when we crossed back through the wall at Checkpoint Charlie to West Berlin, I was staying with our leaders at the rear when one of the older Americans was discovered missing. The German coordinator of the trip, Fritz (there was also a Doktor theologian, Hans, in charge), went back and forth through control until the missing American was discovered blithely enjoying a beer on the western side, having wandered off on his own. We promptly had a few drinks as well; I'll never forget what Fritz said at the bar after his harrowing afternoon as he took a shot of schnapps: "The first one is medicine."

Later that year I went to Israel to volunteer at a peace and reconciliation center in the town of Shefar Am (or Shef Amr in Arabic), the House of Hope, run by my Christian Palestinian friend Elias Jabbour.* His father had been mayor of the town in 1948 on the Day of Independence for Jews, or the Nakba, the "catastrophe," for Palestinians. There was no wall at that time, but when I flew out of Tel Aviv only three days after I had arrived because my brother was killed, I was grilled by the authorities over and over because I was with Arab Israelis. I did not return to Israel for thirty years and have now taken two classes to Israel and Palestine, the West Bank. The stark ugliness of the wall, which the Israelis have labeled a "security fence," caught everyone on the bus by surprise as we road from Jericho up to Jerusalem. It runs like a white snake across the hills around the settlements in the West Bank, east of Jerusalem. But as we drove closer in, we could see the other side, the Palestinian side, from the highway, only one hundred feet away. The buildings were cramped and the ground strewn with rubble. There was graffiti along the Palestinian side but not on the Israeli side, where few Palestinians are allowed to cross. Worst of all was our visit to Hebron to see the Tombs of the Patriarchs and then Rachel's Tomb, in between Jerusalem and Bethlehem. These sites of religious devotion (and struggle, especially Hebron, the site of many incidents of resistance or terrorism, depending on your side) are war zones, strictly controlled by the Israeli military. Access in Hebron is divided between a Muslim and Jewish side. Rachel's Tomb is a Jewish-only site approached on a narrow street with the very high barbed wire "security fence" lining both sides of the street. It's divisive by definition and dehumanizing by design. It fits a Roman concept—"we" are on this side and "you" are on the other. You are a barbarian. It's the wall of apartheid—you don't belong with us. You are not human on that side of the wall. But no, we are all human and we belong together.

Hadrian set lines between Roman and barbarian, two sides where previously there had only been one. Oddly, there were Britons on both sides of Hadrian's Wall, perhaps even from the same tribe, dividing the same people just as a wall on the Mexico-US border would.

---

* Elias passed away from COVID-19 in December 2020. Rest in peace, my friend.

A few years ago, I traveled to Rome to learn more about Hadrian. It was my first trip in over seven years and the city, the monuments, and the food were glorious. I spent a lot of time at two of Hadrian's most famous buildings—the Pantheon in the historical center of Rome and his villa in Tivoli, an hour or so east of the city by local bus.

My growing obsession with the wall made me think it was important to him as well. If walking it was this important to me, it must have been important to him! I was feeling a bond with Hadrian, a kinship. I had read Marguerite Yourcenar's *Memoirs of Hadrian*, a beautiful piece of historical fiction published in 1951. The novel is a long letter to Marcus Aurelius from the dying Hadrian narrating the dying emperor's entire life. Yourcenar has given us Hadrian's voice, and anyone who reads this book will always hear her Hadrian.

We know, from many historical sources and actions he took, that the project of creating boundaries around the empire was important to him. It was part of Hadrian's project of redefining what it meant to be Roman. But his heart was not in northern Britannia. His heart was in the east, where he met a teenage boy who became the love of his life, as we shall see in the next chapter, and at the end of his life, his heart was at his villa in Tivoli, where he recreated the empire with himself at the center. This was the largest Roman villa ever constructed, with thousands and thousands of slaves who worked in underground kitchens and traveled in hidden corridors so Hadrian didn't have to see the people who served him. The villa was his life's work. He designed many buildings, most notably the masterpiece of the Pantheon, and worked on his villa for over twenty years. The wall was but a peripheral boundary for Hadrian, a short walk in Britain before moving on to greater things while his legions carried out his vision in the farthest corner of his empire. He was the emperor of Rome, the most powerful and richest man in the history of the world. He was a God. All the emperors were deified, but Hadrian lived like a God in his villa.

We are all divine in our aspirations if not our deeds. And my deed was God-like, walking across England, solving the problem of my father's suicide after twenty-five years. Making the world whole again, as God promises in the Bible. This is called *tikkum olam* in Hebrew: "repairing the world." This is something we all try, we all should try. And then I hit a dead end because I took a wrong turn, and I'm no God at all, just Bob, who can't get anything right at work no matter how hard he tries.

Today, Hadrian's villa is in ruins.

CURLEWS

≥≤ Mourners

After leaving Britain in 122 with the construction of the wall underway, Hadrian traveled across Roman France, Gaul at the time, to the eastern end of the empire, first to Bithynia, the northern edge of what is now Turkey along the Black Sea, in 123–124, and then on to western Turkey, the Roman province of Asia Minor along the Aegean Sea. It was probably on this visit that he met his lover, a beautiful boy named Antinous who was from the countryside in Bithynia. There is no public record of Hadrian and Antinous together until they were in Egypt in 130, where a poet described them hunting a lion.

> And swifter than the steed of Adrastus
> Which once saved its master as he fled through battle.
> Such was the steed whereon Antinous sat in wait for the deadly lion,
> Holding in his left hand the bridle-rein
> And in his right a spear tipped with adamant.
> First Hadrian his brass fitted spear wounded the beast
> But slew him not, for of purpose he missed the mark,

Wishing to test to the full the sureness of aim
Of his lovely Antinous, son of the Argus-slayer.

While literary sources are brief for Antinous, there are many surviving statues and images of him. Most of these portray Antinous as an idealized teenager, but one, a circular relief or tondo in the Arch of Constantine in Rome, shows him as a young man of about twenty. This could mean that Hadrian and Antinous were together for up to seven years.

Hadrian was not crossing a wall by taking Antinous as a lover. The sexual exploits of emperors such as Caligula and Nero were both infamous and legendary. Trajan, while known as both a virile general and family man, preferred boys in his later years. Hadrian clearly preferred men; today we might call him gay or bisexual, but modern gender identities are foreign to Greco-Roman antiquity. Hadrian's marriage to his wife, Sabina, was political and polite but apparently loveless, and they had no children. Taking a young man for so long did however cross a wall; Hadrian might have been influenced by the ancient Greeks, as he was in so many ways. The elite ancient Greeks maintained the custom of an older man, the "lover" (in Greek, *erastēs*) taking on a younger man, the "beloved" (*erōmenos*), as pupil or protégé as well as sexual partner, as seen famously in Plato's *Symposium*. A year or so before the trip to Egypt, while hunting again in Asia, perhaps with Antinous, Hadrian restored the tomb of Alcibiades, the *erōmenos* or object of affection and devotion for Socrates in the *Symposium*. While Hadrian regularly restored tombs of ancient Greek heroes, perhaps Alcibiades had special significance for him as he traveled the empire with his lover. Hadrian's behavior provoked gossip and criticism in the senate. The highest wall he crossed with Antinous was infatuation— perhaps love, perhaps obsession.

Was Antinous obsessed with Hadrian? Did he return the older man's love as well as his desire? Did he have a choice? That's what I wonder, but it's something we will never know. The emperor of Rome picked him out while visiting Bithynia, perhaps at an athletic competition, maybe during a hunt, or at a banquet where Antinous danced with other boys. Could someone resist or say no to the emperor, to a God? By Greek standards, the relationship was appropriate until Antinous reached manhood. We do know they were together and toured Egypt in 130 as Hadrian continued his way around the empire. There, Antinous committed suicide by drowning himself in the Nile. Again, we do not know why, only when and where. There was some indication of religious ritual around his death, that he was offering himself to the spirit (Lat. *genius*) of Emperor-God Hadrian by taking on the ritual death of Osiris in the Nile. And perhaps he was. Others have speculated that he had to end the relationship when he turned twenty. But from my vantage point, it is hard to see this as anything but a young man's suicide, what we would call today depression.

My father died in May, but the illness began well over a year before. In the autumn of 1990, he was giving dire warnings of a financial crash of apocalyptic magnitude. As graduate students with little income, Anne and I were both apprehensive from his warnings because he was a successful and wealthy lawyer, but also doubtful about his advice to not spend any money at all. My parents visited us in 1990 in New Haven, during a time when he still sounded lucid and had convinced my mother as well that a financial crash to rival the Great Depression was imminent. Keep your bikes and sell your car! he warned us. Our plan to buy a new mattress (we were trying to get pregnant that fall, successfully as it turned out) was met with grave disapproval; *don't spend a penny you don't have to.* Our skepticism started to grow. Anne was studying economics, and while she wasn't focused on markets or the business cycle, rather labor economics (a poor pun since she gave birth the following year), no one at the Yale economics department or school of management was predicting a financial crash. My father's warning was a lonely voice. As it turned out, it was more than that; it was the first cry of pain from a broken man.

We had spent the summer before in Georgia at Stillwaters Farm, where there were two houses. My parents had purchased the original farmhouse and almost twenty acres around the time we were married and added ten or so more acres of mostly woodland when an adjacent parcel went up for sale. This peaceful spot, if quite warm in the summer, included springs that fed a small pond and lake, which was dammed, and tumbled into a nice stream that left the property on the south side. Along with my father-in-law, we built a couple of bridges over the stream. My father was not a builder and didn't participate; perhaps he was working at the office. When he first bought the place, my father called one small field his "dove field," which is a major hunt in the South, but he never hunted. We had a shotgun and rifle and enjoyed occasional skeet and target shooting, as well as protection from water moccasins. The farm was in Pine Mountain Valley, Georgia, not far from Warm Springs, where Franklin Roosevelt visited for polio treatment. FDR liked to drive up Pine Mountain and look out over the valley. The WPA built cottages for his view from the hilltop park during the Great Depression. My parents bought, moved, and renovated a "valley cottage" to their thirty-acre property, situated across the pond from the original house. When the trailer along the drive in to the house went up for sale, they bought that too. Eventually they petitioned the county to change the name of the small lane leading to the houses to Stillwaters Lane, which it remains to this day.

Anne and I spent the summer of 1990 in the new cottage, which was quite a luxury for two graduate students. I tutored elementary school students in Columbus while studying for my language exams in French (by reading "Asterix" comic books, since I was pretty fluent in French) and German (which I never really learned and promptly forgot after the exam) while Anne had a research fellowship from the economics department at Yale. We enjoyed dinners on the new screen porch and occasional nights of love-making on the porch when we pulled the mattress from our bedroom out there for the night, produce from a large garden, and generally a relaxed country life far from the "graduate student ghetto" around Orange Street in New Haven.

The cloud on the horizon was a week at the beach with the family in the beginning of that summer. Years before, when I was in seventh grade, my parents found an island off the tip of Edisto in South Carolina slated for new development, and they bought a lot. The developers went under during the recession in the early '70s, and the island went through a series of owners before, about this time in 1990, a wealthy family in Kentucky purchased it with an agreement with the Nature Conservancy to preserve most of the island for turtle egg nests. When the original development failed, my parents joined several families and self-financed a house on the lot next to ours where a house was barely started before the recession and was sold some time later. Our share meant up to four weeks a year on Botany Bay, in the only house on the island. This was my favorite place in the world growing up: winter walks for hours on deserted beaches, our dog chasing dolphins along the surf, sunsets over the marsh. I visited with friends a few times in college, and there was a family trip soon after Anne and I were married when her father organized an oyster roast on the beach. (The year we were married the first two hurricanes were Anne and Bob. My mother and one younger sister were out on the island and earned t-shirts that said: I survived Hurricane Bob.)

Anne and I made the drive from Columbus to the South Carolina coast, a different and strange route compared to the more familiar roads from Atlanta or Chapel Hill. Armadillos had recently made it to Georgia, and I remember seeing dead ones along the dusty roads south of Macon, where the piedmont I grew up on fell to the coastal plain. We didn't know it would be our last week at Botany Bay. There were walks, body surfing, even helping Nature Conservancy volunteers move turtle eggs. But there was tension, extreme tension, the likes of which I don't ever remember before in family. My mother was very tense and angry that week, lashing out often. One afternoon, I asked what was wrong, and she burst into tears. I asked why and she said it was because someone actually cared how she was feeling.

We left this behind, and I must have ignored or repressed these warning signs. Life at the farm was calm and peaceful: gardening, daily round trips to Columbus to the tutoring center, bike rides at Calloway Gardens. My mother was there much of the time; my father, less frequently. Fixing up the new cottage was like having a new home and not paying for any of it. We enjoyed a few meals out and a party with my parents' new friends in Pine Mountain Valley. The summer culminated in a house-warming party in the cottage, which was fun but again, rather tense. Anne and I drove back to New Haven in August, through Greensboro, North Carolina, where we ordered a new sleeping sofa, a gift from my parents who had spent a weekend in New Haven on the old futon. But when they returned to visit in October, we saw that things were unraveling.

When we went back to Georgia for Christmas two months later, it was clear this financial disaster was still in my father's head and not in our future. We were able to share the news of Anne's pregnancy. The idea of a new grandchild brought some joy, but not enough. He no longer sounded cautious. He was delusional. He was planning to sell the house and move into the trailer at the farm, which was rented out but paid for. I suppose he was planning to sell or rent the farm as well. It didn't make any sense. He had pulled all funds from the stock market and put them in the money markets, anticipating a disaster. No disaster ever happened except the one in his head that he soon brought on himself and our family.

His condition turned to serious, debilitating depression. Sometime in the new year he began psychotherapy, additional counseling, and a brand new drug for depression called Prozac.

After his first suicide attempt in April, I flew to Atlanta to visit him in the hospital. I remember debating this briefly in New Haven because of the cost, but Anne, now five months pregnant, said I had to go. He had brought the shotgun home from the farm. My mother found him on the ground outside the front door, the door we never used except for company. He did not shoot himself, but I think he had taken some drugs and alcohol and passed out. It was the weekend of the Masters, which remains an emotional weekend for me, even though I'm not a golfer. I think it was during this trip that I told my mother we were not planning to name our child "the III" if it was a boy, which we were fairly sure it would be from the nurse's reaction to the ultrasound when we asked if she could tell the gender, even though we didn't want her to tell us. This was not because of my father's illness, more because of Anne's idea of giving names after the mother's side of the family, but that's the way my mother reacted. I don't regret the way we chose names for our son, but I wonder if that bothered her at the time.

During this weekend at home, I spent time in my father's upstairs office, which replaced my high school bedroom. I found files, notes, and drawings he had made in therapy. One drawing showed the course of his life, an upward line with obstacles and a "flat period" at the time of the fatal car accident of my younger brother. Our family drew closer after this, and in many ways, our wedding less than two years after the accident was a celebration of moving forward. Another "flat period" was my sister's divorce about a year after our wedding, so all these major events were fairly fresh in 1991. His line ended in a mass of tangled confusion, a blurry maze like something a child might draw to show anger or fear at being lost. (To be fair, he was terrible at drawing and had to transfer out of an engineering program in college because he couldn't do the drafting required in the 1950s.)

He was calm and controlled at the hospital when I was there, stern or a bit subdued. He was probably ashamed of where he was and me seeing him like this, knowing who he was. He had "acted out" the night before and been restrained—in his words, placed in the padded cell. He seemed both tentative and somewhat proud, even triumphant, at doing this. And angry. My guess is that he had finally found a safe place to break down completely after months or years of pressure at work or at home. The greatest pressure we all face, of course, is from ourselves, and that was certainly true for him. Perhaps screaming and throwing himself around in the "padded cell" was a release from all these pressures, both real and imagined. By that point there was little difference between the two since his very sharp mind had become so clouded by the disease. This was the last time I saw him alive.

At some point in April he abruptly stopped the Prozac, which might have been a catalyst for this or the final suicide attempt. A few weeks later, the Monday after Mother's Day, which was also the day after our wedding anniversary and his own mother's birthday, while my mother was out running errands or at meetings, he connected a hose to the exhaust pipe of his car and put the other end in the rolled-up window. My mother drove in and saw him in the car and knew right away and screamed. Later we learned that he wasn't wearing his wedding ring. It was never found.

I don't remember the phone call or getting to Atlanta. One of his partners picked us up at the airport. My in-laws were there, along with all the family that could make it and many old friends of my parents. The family gathered, talked, and cried in the downstairs study in the house with my parents' longtime therapist. Anne was showing, of course, and we were both afraid of the harm that this stress might bring on but were afraid to talk about it. There was a huge service at St. Anne's, the second funeral for my family in eight years. For the second time, we watched a pine box coffin be driven away from the portico on the northern side of the modern church. I was sobbing, almost uncontrollably. But given an uneven relationship over thirty years, who was I crying for—him or me?

After a funeral, there's a party. The juxtaposition seems odd, but this is a fairly universal human ritual, a celebration meal after a death. For a white family with Midwestern roots, there's not a great deal of difference between a funeral reception and an engagement party. We eat reception food, have drinks, make small-talk. I had a very hard time even coming downstairs for my brother's reception; I remember well my Grandmother Ginny coming upstairs and telling me to get down there and talk to those people. But for my father's reception, I circulated and talked to his old friends from law school and his first job in Evanston, and people I had grown up with in Atlanta. Most were there to support my mother. Some of my high school friends were there too. The former mayor of Atlanta, Maynard Jackson, was at the service, but I don't remember him coming to the house afterward. I do remember talking to one of my father's friends from law school. At some point in the conversation about who knows what, he said "what can you do?" while pointing a finger to his head, mimicking a gun. I don't think the embarrassment of the moment caught up with him before I turned away.

Everyone in the family and everyone who knew him wanted to know: why? Beyond a diagnosis of depression, that's a very hard question to answer. By nature, I want to understand things; I'm an analytical thinker, which probably suits being a professor more than other vocations where you have to make a decision and move on. But I've had a hard time understanding what happened. We know a great deal more about depression and depression medications today than twenty-five years ago, but I'm not sure that would have saved him.

I understand more now, both cognitively and emotionally, from other experiences. Depression is a disease and people suffer from depression like people suffer from cancer and heart disease. Medicine and therapy can help. But shame can be unbearable, if shame it was that led to my father's death. He had to feel shame, I think, to try again to kill himself. In ancient Rome, senators sought and received approval from Hadrian to commit suicide. Honor was a different concept then.

When I planned this walk along Hadrian's Wall, I wasn't thinking about the twenty-fifth anniversary of my father's death, or Antinous. That came later. And there's nothing to connect my father and Antinous except a walk and a wall, an activity and an artifact. But this is what religion does. Religion makes connections and provides meaning; it tries to make sense where things seem senseless. I thought a lot about the walk before I went. But in ways that I hardly anticipated, walking the wall became a meaning-making activity for me.

CHAPTER 5

YELLOWHAMMERS

━ Deceivers

The morning in Corbridge was bright and "fine," as the British would call it, after the gray and gloomy evening. This was the day I would connect with Anne and Ginna for a few days of walking together along the center of Hadrian's Wall Path, which put me in a mood that matched the weather. It would be good to be with family. First I had to negotiate getting up and dressed in my "monk's cell" without banging my head or knees. I already had a blister but luckily wasn't quite as stiff as the morning before. After the Angel's "Full English" in the same restaurant I had dinner the night before, I walked over to Boots the Chemist for plasters to cover my new blister. I packed up and left my gear at the Angel— in the parlor where less hardy walkers had placed their luggage for the services that run suitcases along the path—and walked out to Corbridge Roman Town, one of the Roman forts along the way that preceded the wall. The impressive ruins of the fort date to the Roman general Agricola—rival to Domitian, the last "bad" emperor before Nerva—who tried unsuccessfully to invade Scotland about fifty years before Hadrian built his boundary between Britannia and the north.

On the way to Corbridge, I stopped at St. Andrew's, an Anglo-

Saxon church that shows the strong connection between the wall and the English villages and towns that were built later. It has a Roman arch from the ancient fort over the baptismal font and standing next to the church is a pele tower, a fortified tower built from Roman stones in the eighth century during the Viking invasions. It was later used as a vicarage for the church. I popped in just to see the arch at about 10 a.m. and was greeted by a very kind and quite lovely octogenarian docent. Judging by her keen interest in showing me everything else in the church, my guess is that she doesn't get a lot of business, at least not on a weekday morning. I tried to be polite and took a few pictures of a tombstone in the church floor, which was carved with an outline of a medieval woman next to a pair of shears. I left as quickly as I could. The path along the Tyne was quite pleasant, without a backpack on the way out, and I didn't even turn on my route tracker to log the distance. But taking the shorter route back along the road to the town center after touring the site, I realized I probably should have explored taxi or bus options, given the miles ahead.

I collected my gear at the Angel and enjoyed walking back up the route that I should have taken down to the river valley the day before. The path led through the outskirts of the town and this time under the A90, then crossed a charming ford with a post marked by feet for motor drivers to gauge the height of the brook. The water was low, but I used the small foot bridge and walked up a country lane with high hedges full of goldcrests and yellowhammers, bright and tiny birds with colors that matched their names. Passing the wrong turn from the day before and pausing to take a picture (now I can be relaxed about it!), I continued walking up the hill, past Halton Castle again and its diverse, dirty sheep population. I was back on the ridge of the wall path, which was gray and cold, much different from the warm, sunny valley I had just walked out of.

A few miles along the wall path I reached the Errington Arms, situated between the villages of East Wallhouses and Wall in Northumberland, a pub known for its sandwiches, according to Henry Stedman, my trusty guidebook author. With such a reputation I decided to try the Sea of Love sandwich, which included smoked salmon, prawns, fresh crab, dill, and crème fraiche. Delicious. The pub lies at the modern roundabout where the A68 crosses the B6318, the Military Road, and marks the Roman Port Gate, where ancient Dere Street ran south to York and north to Scotland, one of the few gates in Hadrian's Wall. I sat for a while, charging my phone and chatting with the barkeep, resting up for the afternoon ahead, until about 2:30.

After lunch, the weather turned much colder. Soon, I was walking through vallum deep enough to hide a sheep—so the locals say, and there were a lot of sheep. I ducked into the vallum for a quick change of shirts, visible only to the omnipresent sheep, and had to put on my jacket for a while as the path carried forward through the bumpy outlines of abandoned medieval quarries, a plantation of conifers that had been recently harvested, and sections of swampy ditch. It was all kind of spooky as the weather went dark and cloudy. I was heading for a tearoom at St. Oswald's Hill Head before turning south again to Acomb.

But the weather cleared again, which I celebrated by overshooting my rest stop and the left turn south by a half-mile. I had to hike that half-mile back up the hill to St. Oswald's, another Anglo-Saxon church marking the battle of Heavenfields. According to the Venerable Bede in his *History of the English People* (731 CE), this is the field where the Anglo-Saxon and, more importantly for Bede, Christian King Oswald defeated the pagan Celtic King Cadwalla and his allies. Oswald had a vision the night before from the Irish St. Columba, the founder of Iona in Scotland, and he gathered his army around a cross in this field for the battle. Either Oswald, or more likely Bede, knew the story of Emperor Constantine at the Battle of the Milvian Bridge. Constantine's vision of the cross in 312 CE—"in this sign you will conquer"—the night before the battle for control of Rome led to the legalization of Christianity in the Empire. Oswald went on to spread Christianity in the north of England. After his death, the saint's body was divided up and his head went to Lindisfarne, Holy Island, and the mother church of English Christianity in the north. St. Oswald's church has a fine if somewhat incongruous Roman altar against the wall behind all the pews. I met a couple who had just finished the walk from Lindisfarne—St. Oswald's Trail. We chatted briefly, and I took pictures of the graveyard as well as the church, which turned out dramatically as black and white images against the gray sky.

Leaving the churchyard, I found the proper route leading south down a lane from the large cross marking the battlefield. After a few houses on the right, I went through a gate onto a farm track, but soon reached another gate leading to a large field. My guidebook didn't include very clear directions: "just cross sheep field straight south." *Henry, you're letting me down now!* While the initial path was fairly clear, I was soon guessing between sheep trails and ditches without any clear sense of direction except going downhill and worrying about a repeat of the wrong turn from the day before. But I made the right guess at a gate leading through a field full of yellow rapeseed flowers in full bloom—the source of canola oil—which left bright pollen on my clothes because the path was so narrow. After this field I reached a green gate that signaled, in my guidebook, that I was indeed on the correct path to Acomb. *OK, Henry, I forgive you this time.*

I continued down a road, keeping close watch for a left turn back to the walking path, which I soon found, along with a sign that read: Bull in Field. My guidebook noted this farmhouse was "guarded by highland cattle." Hmmm. What are highland cattle like? Friendly? Fierce? I had no idea. I eyed the cattle in my binoculars and determined they were in fact cows. But what about that one? I stood there a long time deciding what to do. I crossed the stile over the fence and walked down through the field when "that one" walked in my direction with clear interest in my doings. He started to head me off, and I moved up the hill, and he started running. (OK, running, not charging, but it felt like he was charging. He was a real bull!) I decided to retreat, wisely, and climbed back over the fence. I went down the road to the other side of the farmhouse, where I could see the footpath exit at the southern end of the same field. The only way to stay on the path was to get back in that field with the bull. This was the only way not to get lost again.

Casting my previous caution to the wind, I decided to climb over the fence here below the farmhouse, which I hoped would hide me from Mr. Bull. Tossing my pack and poles over first, I hoisted myself over one line of barbed wire to the top of a new wooden fence from which I could jump down. I warily crossed the field, now hidden from the bull by a hillock and a few trees next to the farmhouse driveway. Or perhaps he was still monitoring the northern entrance against the intruder? Without any further encounter, I was on to the next field and safe from the charging bull. This field had a crop, not cattle. Phew!

I continued down the path to a creek and up steps into a street of semi-detached houses in Acomb. I had no clue where to go. A bit of wandering and a question to a lady in her house, and I eventually found the Sun Pub and Inn, where Anne and Ginna were waiting for our family reunion. Our rooms were above the pub, so I got to enjoy a post-bull pint while soaking my tired feet, a sign of pain to come. I had walked over eleven miles, without counting the round trip to Corbridge in the morning. Ginna took a picture of me soaking with the caption "And then I climbed over the barbed wire fence." We had a delightful dinner at the Miner's Arms across the street with a server who seemed to be channeling Hugh Grant while my family caught me up on their visit to Liverpool for a Beatles' tour.

Finishing a nice long bike ride recently, I saw two boys playing golf with two men—fathers or uncles perhaps. The boys were wearing matching sport shirts and shorts. This was not my childhood. My father must have taught me to throw a football and baseball at some point, but I don't remember ever playing any sports with him. We probably tossed the ball a bit when I was younger, but he did not play with any of the children at all. His nephews in Johnson City, Tennessee, liked to play touch football in a vacant lot when we visited for Thanksgiving. There were four boys and an older niece, so his sister had five kids, just like us. We had one, and only one Christmas together, if I remember correctly. There were ten sick kids in our house in Atlanta that December, and I'm pretty sure my parents decided never to do it again. Once or twice there was a family touch football game over at the elementary school near our house.

My father was a fine athlete during high school in Danville, Illinois, where he was starting quarterback and the basketball point guard. He remained active until he was fifty-seven, when he started to get depressed. He joined in the tennis craze of the 1970s, which he played very well, and continued to play for most of the rest of his life. He turned to jogging with the rest of the country in the 1980s. He did many 10K races in Atlanta, often with younger law associates who finished the race exhausted while he turned around and ran back home. The half-marathon was a comfortable distance for him. He ran three marathons—one in Georgia; the London marathon in 1984 when Anne and I were over there after our post-college year; then the New York City Marathon while Anne and I were living in DC after we were married and before graduate school, I think 1986. But marathons tended to wipe him out.

I did not find my stride as an athlete until high school and even adulthood. Football and baseball were not for me like they had been for my father. I always felt he was ashamed that I wasn't a typical American-style athlete. Once I asked him about substitution rules in a baseball game—I know I was younger than eight because we were in the old house we lived in before my little sisters were born. "At your age I could name every starting player in the Majors, and you don't know the rules?" It was mean and sarcastic. How would I know if he didn't teach me? He could be that way.

I played a year of football in maybe second or third grade and must have hated it. I played soccer once, I think, and baseball in sixth grade. They were afternoon games, and I always developed a headache. My mother came or dropped me off, but I don't remember my father ever coming. I was OK because I was a fast sprinter and could steal a base pretty easily. No power but I could hit. Sometimes I wish I had tried track because I think I could have done well at the 100 or 200. We all had tennis lessons in the 1970s, and I kept playing but was never particularly good at it. (Anne is a fine tennis player.) I tried football one more time, in eighth grade, and karate a year or two later. For both football and karate, my mother made me buy the cheapest equipment we could find, hardly an endorsement of my abilities. It was a little embarrassing, the small shoulder pads in football, but I wasn't very big, and there was no reason I should ever have been a lineman. But karate was humiliating. I moved through to the yellow belt easily, as most people do, and then it was time to spar with pads. The studio sold pads, but my mother thought they were too expensive. I found some sporting goods supply store, I think in downtown Atlanta. I guess I called around because this was decades before the internet and online ordering. I drove down myself to get them. The first night in the studio, the mild-mannered instructor noticed my different pads and asked to show them to the class. He then went into a fairly detailed explanation about why these were a problem to use and didn't belong there. I never went back.

I developed an early gift for swimming and swam all six years of junior high and high school. My parents never came to a swim meet the entire time I was in high school even though I earned three varsity letters. My father thought, I was told later by my mother, that his parents pressured him too much growing up, and he wanted to give me space. But there's no way a teenager is going to interpret his absence except as uncaring or embarrassed of me. My swimming was hampered by not going to early morning practices in high school until one time in December of a super-busy senior year, while the ensemble was doing a concert every night and we were all finishing college applications. I promptly got very sick for Christmas.

I also ran cross-country for my last two years of high school. My friend Holt and I were always last. He was a best friend with the best singing voice in our class of boys. He became a star in a co-ed acappella singing group at Yale. I might have been a sprinter, but I'm very slow compared to true cross-country runners, but it got me in shape for swim season, and I enjoyed running in the cool fall weather of Atlanta. I saw my first real girlfriend-to-be while running one afternoon in September. I already had had my eye on her, and things got hot pretty quickly soon after that. I asked her out after an informal gathering with classmates one Saturday in a park—the guys were throwing footballs, which I avoided trying. I can't remember if we had beer then. Things were very loose in the '70s, pre-Nancy Reagan and MADD, and the legal age was eighteen, so it was easy to get beer in high school. I know our first date included a six-pack and staying out way past midnight and returning home to find an angry, and now I understand very frightened, mother who thought I had been in an accident. In the shock of the moment— maybe 2 a.m.—I somehow managed to drop the beer in the slide-out garbage drawer and retrieve it later. She, called Sissy by her family but not me, and I never actually did the full deed, but did almost everything else a teen could try, so my first sexual experiences kept me pretty darn close to her that year. Parents weren't a problem because I had a key to a room at church where we spent hours on weekend nights, exploring each other's bodies. But she broke up with me at the end of our junior year when her college-aged other boyfriend came home.

I was completely devastated that summer; it was a true infatuation, and I certainly was going to miss the sex. I moved on, of course, and was super active my senior year, including as one of sixteen singers in the ensemble, the highest honor at school for vocalists. I was also class president of the boys and the front page editor of the newspaper. All of this, and top ten grades earned me a merit scholarship to Chapel Hill. My social circle changed from the "bad" boys and those who went to cool parties to more sedate and smarter friends—although we all shared plenty of beer. I turned eighteen that year, in February, and three other editors of the newspaper who were all at the top of our class brought a case of beer to school for me and then told someone—the Dean of Students?—that a certain unnamed Morehead scholar had a case of beer in his locker. The administration generally was slack with good students and the Heineken came home.

Sissy must have eventually broken up with the college boyfriend—Bret, I think, a name I still don't like very much. She also went to the University of North Carolina, and we talked some our freshman year. I might have even tried to re-kindle what was lost, briefly. At some point she met Anne, who liked her a lot. Meanwhile, Holt was rocketing to acappella fame at Yale; someone once asked him if he was the best tenor on campus, to which he replied, "perhaps." But two or three auditions for me failed to land a spot in the acappella group in Chapel Hill.

I continued to run for almost the next forty years, but I didn't quite make it past fifty-five as a runner, let alone fifty-eight. I ran quite a bit in my twenties, for a few years with work buddies in DC before I went to graduate school. This was the barbaric 1980s, and we didn't have a gym, shower, nap rooms, snacks, or free meals, perks that my millennial son has enjoyed for years at high tech companies and start-ups. But we had a fantastic rail-trail behind the office park. We sponged off in the men's room, which I remember really grossed my father out. He couldn't imagine not showering after his runs. He was able to run in the morning, something I've never really taken on.

Grad school was designed by some hellish committee to make young adults feel tense and insecure. I found that running and walking our dog in the parks around New Haven relaxed me during very tense times. I guess I knew at the time that it was better to bend than to break, but I wasn't very good at putting that into practice. I did know that I was making choices different from my other college friends who were lawyers or doctors already. Holt, for instance, is a successful urologist in Atlanta.

By my twenties I realized that going from A to B fast or long, or both, was really good for more than my strength and waistline. I caught the runner's high. No softball or basketball league for me, just running. I sometimes ran with my father after college, usually in Atlanta while we were on break. Christmas was always warm there, and we often ran together. This was not an all-American father-son game of catch experience; I never had that with my father. I've felt that most strongly when I came to Wabash, and I realized I was looking for a father figure with a couple of authority figures—my first chair, one of the deans. Sometimes I attended the Catholic church with my father on Christmas Day in Atlanta once he converted. And I remember at least one time running with him in the summer in New Haven, maybe right after I received my first degree at the divinity school. My parents visited fairly regularly, as did Anne's parents. We didn't have any money, so vacations were always to their houses or the farm, and we would always go out for a nice dinner when they came to New Haven.

My parents became particularly fond of an eccentric, one-man Chinese restaurant called Peter Cheng's China Garden. This is how the *New York Times* review from 1985 starts off:

> Dining at Peter Cheng's in New Haven forces you to determine your dining priorities. If you want to enjoy some of the most remarkable Chinese food you will find in any Chinese restaurant in Connecticut, then welcome! Here the food is the star. This is not a place of candlelight, fresh flowers on a well-napped table, or seductive decor. It is just the opposite. The decor is nondescript, there are long delays between courses and the entire dinner can stretch to two and a half hours.

It was worth it. The food was extraordinary indeed. We got to know Peter, a bit. And we spent a lot of time in the restaurant enjoying our meal. My mother is a "restaurant talker"—actually, she's a "stranger talker"—the source of much embarrassment growing up. My siblings and I coined a phrase, "trading recipes," for what happened between her and the chef by the end of every dinner out. (That's me now, at a lot of restaurants.) But everywhere we went she talked to strangers for longer than she usually talked to us. Anyway, we got into a long conversation with Peter one night on our third visit or so. I remember he said, "a good chef loves to eat," which is true of me. I looked him up, and he died at the ripe old age of eighty-eight. The obituary reported that he was a "follower of Christ" for forty years; now that I think about it, my mother and Peter talked about church as well.

It was while we were still in graduate school in New Haven that my father died. I was in the first year of the Ph.D. program, having received full tuition and a nice fellowship from the Episcopal Church Foundation. I don't remember when I started running again after his death; the summer is a blur now. Nolen was born only a few months later, in August. We had a new puppy as well, named Emmy Lou after the singer, a Chesapeake Retriever like the unfortunate Molly. I walked, every day, the half-mile down to East Rock Park fields on the south side of the Mill River. Nolen rode in the stroller or, on many snowy days, the backpack. Emmy Lou, who we paid to have trained after she tossed a toy in Nolen's crib one day, was an awesome Frisbee catcher for almost her whole life of fourteen years. She caught the Frisbee in the sun and the snow, and we attracted a lot of attention. This went on for two years in New Haven, although I can't remember how long I could carry Nolen in the backpack.

We moved to Stanford the summer of 1993. In the East Rock Park playground, there was a fun shaking bridge for kids that I told Nolen was getting him ready for earthquakes. Stanford campus is ideal for runners. When I first arrived, I could run up in the hills to the famous Stanford Dish, a landmark radio telescope in the beautiful foothills that surround the western side of "the farm," as they call Stanford. Ginna was born three years after we moved, which slowed me down a bit. She never got the amount of walking in Stanford that Nolen did in New Haven. We only had one car and bought a Burley bike trailer so I could ride Nolen, and eventually both of them, to the child care coop on my way to or from the library. I added a wheel to turn it into a running stroller, which I did fairly often the year Ginna was born. (Once, in an "only-at-Stanford" accident, a woman in a golf cart crashed into the trailer while it was parked at the coop. The cause of the accident was a broken foot. She bought us a new trailer).

Once, I took a bad fall and scraped my hands, quite ugly; Ginna, not even a year old then, was fine. I remember this because a classics professor I had worked for as a teaching assistant in the old Stanford CIV (Cultures, Ideas, and Values) program for first-year students ("frosh" in Stanford-speak), asked me to do a continuing ed class on the history of the Apocalypse, which I called Apocalypse Then, Apocalypse Now. I had done a five-week class on the Letters of Paul, very fun and successful, the year before around the time Ginna was born in April. The classics professor had a weekly interview show on the Stanford community television channel for continuing ed, and he invited me for a show. I brought a large book of apocalyptic images from art and architecture and, at one point, the camera zoomed in on my disgusting, scabby fingers pointing out some aspect of the picture, maybe Albrecht Dürer's *Four Horsemen*. The class did not get enough people to run.

A year later I had my second serious lower back problem, spasms for months and no teaching the entire spring quarter. Stanford was generous with disability and the wife of one of my co-teaching fellows, the now-renowned archaeologist Eric Cline, was able to fill in for me—the historian Diane Cline, now a professor at George Washington University. People asked me if I had gained weight to cause the back problem, and I pointed at Ginna and said, "Yeah, twenty-five pounds." We lived in a Stanford dorm that year and the next as resident fellows. This paid for food and housing, a big deal in Palo Alto, while we rented our condo to a recently widowed scientist from France named Patrice and his two young sons. After the lower back injury, running was off the schedule for several years until we moved to Crawfordsville. I was still under forty and able to spring back over the next few years and put in more serious miles in the flat Indiana landscape. Serious, but slow. Once I got going I could keep going, but I began to notice that my acceleration was fading to almost non-existent. I slowed like a freight truck turning corners on the streets.

The last road race I ran was in Crawfordsville, at the Strawberry Festival in June of the summer we moved. I knew everyone there over forty that morning. *I'm going to win my age group!* I said to myself, *because there's no one else here in my age group!* And then my colleague Dennis the physicist showed up. I came in second in my age group. Dennis is still running—I see him around Crawfordsville when I'm driving in or out—but I am not. I kept running in Zionsville for a five years, but once we went on sabbatical to Harlaxton, the trip that spurred the big walk along the wall, I was struggling with achy knees and lower back and started focusing on cycling for my exercise, which I love. And there is freedom on a long bike ride, knowing you are way out on a country road all by yourself, that you got there all by yourself and have to get back home on your own. There is an aerobic rush for me as well, the runner's high that kicks in on a bike after about ten miles.

But it wasn't until I decided to walk Hadrian's Wall that I discovered this freedom again, a walker's high during those first few days along the trail.

Running, and now cycling or hiking, eases anxiety, which I am much more subject to than depression. Anxious about the passage of time, opportunities missed, decisions made. I remember feeling this way at the beach the summer before we were at the farm when my parents were fighting and my father was getting sick. And in England the summer after graduation from college. In New Haven, when I had to decide whether to accept an offer for the Ph.D. program or roll the dice again with a master's program in the hopes of getting more financial aid; then I felt physically sick. And when our family traveled after the sabbatical semester teaching at Harlaxton in England the year before the walk, I went through a period of tremendous anxiety over our son back at home, who had been having a very rough time with his own depression. This led me to therapy, medication for a brief time, and eventually meditation and yoga. And I was able to tell the story of running from the police to my freshman class.

Running and walking help me but weren't enough for my father. I won't ever know exactly what was going on the year or so before my father killed himself. Something went wrong, and he couldn't get over it. Was it the hint of malpractice in the lawsuit? If so, he couldn't move on. He couldn't bend. It's very hard to do. Adapting on the fly while on a glorious walk across England is a lot easier than bending and adapting in day-to-day life. Maybe he tried to run away, and he should have tried walking.

I remember a camping trip in Wisconsin with Dad and my younger brother John. I might have been eleven. My grandmother died the year after I turned twelve. My grandparents had a country house among farms in Wisconsin where my mother had spent her summers with uncles and a grandmother who farmed the area. My grandfather had been a doctor in Chicago, self-taught after being orphaned at age twelve, and he built this house where his wife's family had come from. They retired there before I was born. Anyway, we went camping near the farm, my father and brother and me, a bonding experience that ended up going south. I'm not sure why. I don't really like camping now, but I don't remember a lot of bad going on, and I do remember having some fun with my brother. Did we fish? My parents had camped before we were born, and our earliest beach trips involved camping in Florida and South Carolina. We were using the same Sears canvas tent in Wisconsin, one of those huge family tents. The bad memory happened one morning when my father decided—announced? ordered?—that we were going hiking. I didn't want to. We didn't want to? I can't remember where my brother stood on this, my brother who died thirty-three years ago in a car driven by a drunk driver. We got in a fight. I remember my father yelling, "We are going on a hike!" I wonder if there were tears. I can imagine his side of this now, which must have been hard for a father. You've taken a side and drawn a line and want to stick to the plan, but you might also feel you're being too harsh and can't find a way out of it.

Did we ever go? Did I get sick to get out of it? To get out of camping? I said I felt bad and ended up in bed at the farmhouse. My grandfather said I had a fever. I am not sure I did. I might have faked it to get out of camping or hiking or even being with my father. He was very disciplined and never very flexible. When the blow of the lawsuit fell, he was not able to bend.

CHAPTER 6

SKYLARKS

🦅 Singers

After three days of walking the trail, I thought I'd never need my warm hat and gloves. I was wrong.

Backing up a bit, Anne and Ginna had met up in London a few days earlier and then did a Beatles tour of Liverpool before taking the train to Hexham and a taxi to meet me in Acomb. The three of us were to walk the center of Hadrian's Wall Path together for next three days, much shorter walks which my aching feet greatly appreciated. Walking with my family was also the center of my trip. I had pushed pretty hard to get here in three days, with a late start, wrong turns, and of course a bull. The next three days were planned to be light and relatively easy.

The next morning, after our enjoyable and delicious reunion dinner, we set off in a cab around 10:30 on a gray morning with packed lunches from our inn and rejoined the trail right where I had turned around the day before below Heavensfield. While I was a stickler for walking every inch of the route, Anne and Ginna didn't see any reason to spend time walking up the hill to Hadrian's Wall. We were rewarded with early wall sightings at Planetrees, where the thickness changes from the "broad wall" I had seen at Heddon-on-Wall on my second day to the smaller wall on the broader, original three-meter foundations, and shortly after that, Brunton Turret, the best-preserved turret on the path, in the middle of lovely farmland where the wall comes in from the east "broad" and heads out to the west "narrow." The Roman legions and I felt the need for a break in the hard work at about the same point along the wall heading east to west.

Leaving the field surrounding Brunton Turret and its sheep (the sheep became a focus of Anne and Ginna's photography, including many "sheep selfies," for the next three days), we followed a lane back onto the busy B6318 Military Road, leading across the River North Tyne. Unfortunately, the path to the surviving Roman bridge abutment on the south bank of the river, which apparently features the finest Roman carved phallus on the entire path, was closed. We stopped at Riverside Tearooms on the other side of the modern bridge for morning refreshment, which was a nice sign of an easier pace that had eluded me to this point. As we left, the temperature was dropping and we put on warmer clothes and followed the B6318 to the entrance and car park of the magnificent Chesters Roman Fort.

This beautifully excavated fort boasts probably the finest Roman bathhouse in Britain. It's down by the river where you can see the Roman bridge that we missed on the southern bank, and no, even with binoculars, I couldn't spot the phallus. The ruins of the fort are fully excavated in the midst of lush lawns that clearly show the size of the buildings and the distances between them. There are more complete forts, at Vindolanda and Housesteads, but the contrast between stone and grass at Chesters is striking. The path leading to the fort has four stone plaques set in the ground along the way with historical quotations about Hadrian and the wall, from Hadrian's biographer in 400 CE: "Hadrian was the first to construct a wall, eighty miles in length, which was to separate the Romans from the barbarians"; and the Venerable Bede in 731: "The Romans built a strong wall from sea to sea. This famous wall is still to be seen"; and from Victorian-era explorers and restorers, including the notable John Clayton on Chesters: "These remains of Roman luxury have lain undisturbed for 1400 years."

You can't spend too much time on Hadrian's Wall without running into John Clayton's work. He was a nineteenth-century clerk and amateur archaeologist in Newcastle who inherited an estate that included the fort and baths at Chesters. He eventually bought four of the forts and restored quite a bit of the wall. After lunch, I toured his extraordinary, over-stuffed Victorian museum of Roman antiquities, which sits behind the modern visitor's center. The museum is so full that there are large red plaques with the words Curator's Choice on selected objects, so you don't have to study every slab, stele, or statue to find the best ones.

We stayed for well over an hour, eating lunch down by the river in the well-preserved *sudatorium*, which was the very hot, dry sweat room of the baths, with walls that sheltered us from the wind. After we toured the museum and I tried on a Roman soldier kit, which they sell and use for reenactments of Roman soldiers on summer weekends with children and grown men acting like children, we headed back out to the road from the car park, through construction and then up a steep hill to a beautiful view east and finally a trail through fields. We had been walking uphill the entire way from Chesters when we reached the fields of sheep—lots of sheep. There were good views of the Roman ditch until we approached the next wall sighting at Black Carts. By then it was getting really cold. At lunch we had added a layer of vests, and I had changed my hat to a stocking cap and put on gloves. We went up some steps to a stile and paused to watch a kestrel hovering in the north wind, then, passing the outline of Milecastle 29, crossed into Black Carts, named for a farm up the lane. This stunning stretch of wall and ditch, includes another fine turret, 29A. This turret was built before the wall came this far west and it has projecting "broad wall" wings that are connected to "narrow" curtain wall. It is also perfectly placed so as to have a spot to hide from the wind and pull out warmer clothes. As we left the stretch of wall, we chatted with folks going the other way, suggesting they take a break in the turret from the wind. We continued onward and upward, with gloves on our hands and hoods fastened tightly around hats.

The wall faded, and I found the transition to unexcavated wall as interesting as the unexcavated forts I had seen the first three days of walking. There's something about the suggestiveness of the hillocks, the bits of wall rising from the ground and then disappearing into a wall-shaped mound. The sharp ditch was still north of the unexcavated wall, and rows of yellow gorse lined the path, their bright color highlighting the grayness of the stones and the skies. Soon, we reached Limestone Corner, where the Romans pitched partially dressed stones into the defensive ditch. The whinstone here was too tough to cut, so they moved on. This is also the northernmost point of the wall.

The Romans, with help from the weather, won the day by breaking apart our little family walking group in the last mile or two. I was stopping frequently to take pictures—I took hundreds during the nine days of the walk. Since this meant standing in the cold wind, Anne wanted to go ahead to our bed and breakfast, which was right on the wall path. Ginna wanted to do both—she's done a lot of backpacking trips and was enjoying her first day out—but her legs were freezing at this point. As we approached the partially excavated Roman fort of Brocolitia, which I wanted to explore, they went ahead. The mist had also turned to light rain. I walked around the fort for a while, then down to the Mithraeum. This was the part of the wall we had stopped at when in the car two years before, and I was the only one who went to the Mithraeum while Anne and my brother-in-law Brian stayed in the car. Clearly, the hold of the Romans is limited, but I enjoyed the cold rain as I finished the day's walk. I had anticipated a King Lear moment on the walk, while the furious elements tested me for hours with rain, wind, lightning, and maybe even rolling boulders while I shouted at the elements. But it turned out to be a pretty light test since the bed and breakfast was only fifteen minutes from the mithraeum in the drizzle. But I was getting my experience of the wall in true English weather. I was with my family. The inn ahead promised to be one of the nicest we would stay in. I was happy.

We enjoyed a wonderful meal and a beautiful, large family room that night at Carraw with a view of the moors to the south, dusky gray in the long evening and pale gray-green in the misty morning. The weather stayed wet and overcast, which, along with a luxurious bed, helped me have the best sleep of the walk since the sun and the birds didn't start up at 4 a.m. After a fine breakfast, we walked around the inn to rejoin the wall path, quickly donning caps and gloves again. It was misty, drizzly cold all day with strong northern winds. There were many more walkers in both directions here at the wall path's center; we walked quite slowly and were passed regularly. At one point, a spontaneous group meeting of parties heading both directions converged on the path and we traded plans and itineraries. The second half of the short day was very steep and rugged, with some of the best preserved milecastles and turrets so far as well as segments of damp wall and the often muddy ditch leading into sections of unexcavated wall. We passed Sewingshields Farm and the Sewingshields Wood behind it, with many birds, sky larks, and chaffinches calling in the shelter of the wet trees as we neared. The ditch disappeared at the first of many crags to come, with steep rocky slopes on the northern side. The trail, which stayed on the south side of the wall, was not dangerous, but the rocky cliffs on the north fell precipitously into the clouds. The Romans didn't need a ditch here at all.

We ended the day with a very slow walk across the dramatic approach to Housesteads fort along the misty crag, passing a copse of trees in a ruined milecastle, an Anglo-Saxon tomb built into the wall, and muddy Knag Burn Gate, added by the Romans in the fourth century for locals traveling north and south. All three of us walked down the hill and ate our packed lunch from Carraw B&B outside the Housesteads visitor's center café, overlooking the car park. The weather and the Romans divided us again. Ginna took my full pack, and she and Anne walked to the nearby farmhouse B&B, Beggar's Bog, while I went back up the hill to the Roman fort.

The gate behind the visitor's center was guarded by several sheep, but they retreated as I passed through and walked up the hill to the fort. Housesteads was the fourth stamp on my passport. I enjoyed visiting the museum leisurely this time, unlike Segendunum on the first day when I was anxious to get started; it was also a nice spot to dry out. There was plenty of time on this short day and it was warm and dry in the small building. The animated film about the Roman fort was narrated by Theoden from *Lord of the Rings*, the actor Benard Hill. I went back outside to photograph the well-preserved fort with my waterproof GoPro. Just outside the fort is a sixteenth-century Bastle House, a fortified farm house built partially out of the original Roman gate. I didn't take a photo because I had a nice one from two years before when the weather was unnaturally warm and sunny for October. I remembered looking at the wall path to the west of Housesteads, off the corner of the fort leading into a small copse of trees. I have sunnier pictures from both corners of Housesteads. I even climbed the wall of the fort to see farther west, which was a pretty tall jump down, and what it would be like to walk Hadrian's Wall Path. Tomorrow we would continue on that path.

The drizzle was turning into a more consistent light rain, so I walked back down the hill amongst the flocks of sheep, through the visitor's center and short way back on the road to the B&B for a shower and to wash my clothes. We had the annex behind the old farmhouse, which turned out to be about as bad as Carraw was good the night before. While there were great views across the fields from the driveway, the host didn't turn on the heat until Anne and Ginna arrived and it was still cold when I got there (both Anne and Ginna were in their beds after taking a hot bath). Our room was tiny and the Wifi didn't reach back there, although there was a television. We didn't want to watch television.

The host drove us to the Twice Brewed Pub in Once Brewed. The story is that General Wade, while either building his Military Road or chasing Bonnie Prince Charlie, complained about the beer here, and it had to be brewed again. We had a decent meal and enjoyed the internet for a few hours. The pub was chockfull of walkers, including many other Americans. They were mostly wall walkers since many parties had the same guidebook I was using, although the north-south Pennine Way crosses here as well, which we would see on the path the next day. I think the pub's fame is less from the name or the food, but because it's the only place around with rooms for hikers and next to a hostel and a campground, all pretty much at the center of Hadrian's Wall. It took us a while to get served and then it was difficult to get an expensive taxi back to our B&B at 9:00. I was pretty grumpy about the evening—the room, the cold, the food, the service, the taxi home. But that's the adventure of a rural trek for you. I slept well until the early light woke me for a new day.

It should be clear by now that I was not fond of our host. He was a skinny, intense man, recently divorced and sharing custody of their daughter; he rode a motorcycle, enjoyed rock climbing, and complained about his neighbors. Breakfast was fine, not only because we had the internet in the farmhouse and the views to the south from the drive were exceptional. Since I had an equally good view from our spacious and luxurious room the night before, I really wondered why we were paying just as much. Since we had another short day planned, he suggested we make for Milecastle Inn for lunch—he clearly didn't want to make one for us, even though we would pay, because he had a lot to do around his farm—and we foolishly agreed. He said we would easily be there before 2, and as it turned out we didn't get there until about 3:45. But that's the end of the story of day six.

We walked one mile back up the road, through the visitor's center one last time, and up to Housesteads in cloudy conditions. They let walkers through without a ticket to the fort, and we backtracked part of our route from the day before, walking behind the fort on the north side this time with the cliffs to our right. As the day turned warmer, we began to see long stretches of Clayton's Wall, reconstructed by John Clayton of Chesters where we'd been two days before. We thought it was a steep climb, but it only got steeper across crag after crag. There was no ditch all day among the dramatic crags and best views of the walk so far, labeled "most famous or iconic views of wall" by my guidebook. For hours we saw a series of loughs—lakes—north of the trail. This was the heart of Northumberland National Park, which we had entered two days before in the cold near Blackcarts Farm.

But our chance of a pub lunch was fading. We walked even slower on the hills than we had the day before since Anne, who had a hip replacement the summer before, struggled a bit going up and even more coming down the small but very steep hills. We passed the picture-perfect stone houses of Hotbank Farm, owned by the National Trust, and walked up the steep Highshield Crags overlooking peaceful Crag Lough. Here we paused for a brief snack and a fairly long rest, looking down on the water of the lough. The skies were gray, but it was dry and slowly warming up. A group of young children ran past us going the other way, one or two at a time for what seemed like ten or fifteen minutes. Given the height of the cliffs behind us and the steep downhill ahead of them, we were pretty worried. Eventually, a few adults followed the children. The cliff was steep; they were running and skipping, and we could imagine a terrible tumble.

Two older British men on a day-hike stopped to talk to us right when we were getting ready to head off again. We chatted a bit about our walk and where we were from in America, which most of the British wanted to know. Indiana is a hard one for many people in Britain unless they are

74

basketball or racing fans, so I often say I'm "near Chicago," which is a three-hour drive from my home, but these men had visited America and knew where Indiana was. And then, since it was the summer of 2016, they asked THE question: "What do you think about Donald Trump?" I imagine we looked horrified while assuring them that we strongly opposed him. Trump had just secured the GOP nomination that month, but even conservatives in the UK were speaking out against his racist and xenophobic statements, so I never worried about offending someone with my views in England. The other man said, "There's an American couple we just passed, from Orlando, and she's a Trump supporter." Seeing our dismay, he then looked over the sheer cliff to the lough and said, "This might not be a bad place on the trail to get rid of a Trump supporter." It was the hardest laugh since dinner in Acomb with our charming server. We got their picture—but not their names, unfortunately—and headed in the direction of the couple from Orlando. We ended up passing each other on a very steep downhill for us and uphill for them, almost a vertical climb on the first of several stairs over the hills. The woman dropped her hat while climbing up, which fell about thirty feet. Ginna was going first, and she grabbed it and brought it back up to her. It was only after we had moved on that we realized this was the woman the men were talking about. Perhaps we should have left the hat for her to get on her own, which seemed to fit the attitude of her chosen candidate.

After Crag Lough, the trail began a U-shaped pattern of small hills with very steep ups and downs, often with stairs or near-climbs. The clouds were breaking up, and the sun started to peak through. We came to Sycamore Gap at the bottom of this first U, named after the lone Sycamore tree that stands just south of the wall. The tree gained fame, or notoriety, in an important scene with Kevin Costner in *Robin Hood*. The search for location shots for the film had Robin and his Merry Men all over England, from Kent to Northumberland. It's 175 miles from Sherwood Forest to this tree on Hadrian's Wall, which would be a three-hour drive today, but a good bit longer journey in 1194.

As we approached the Steel Rig parking lot, where many tour buses and day hikers park at what has been called the most beautiful car park in Britain—and indeed the sun was now shining—we realized there was no way we would make it to the pub. More hikers and groups of schoolchildren were passing us going the other way. Our last hope was for a caravan at the car park with tea, rolls, and sandwiches, as you often see in Britain at the little laybys along the highways, but all we found was a toilet—though much appreciated. The realization struck that this was truly going to be a day without lunch. Ginna pointed out that, at our speed, we would never have made it before the pub closed, so why didn't we get sandwiches? (Our pace had slowed from about thirty-six minutes a mile on our first day walking together to well over forty minutes a mile in the steep hills.) I remembered with some longing the sandwiches for sale at the Housesteads Visitors Center we had walked through only three hours before. It was about 1:30. I did a lot of mental browbeating as we walked ten minutes farther up to the highest point on the wall, Green Slack on the Winshield Crags, which would have been an ideal spot for a picnic lunch. The overcast sky was now puffy clouds and sunshine. As it turned out, we had bananas, a couple of Cliff bars, a leftover piece of cake from dinner the night before, and a bag of crisps. My guidebook reported that this was some of the purest air in England, according to the lichen able to grow at this spot. Thankful that we had hoarded some snacks, our spirits rose, perhaps buoyed by the fresh air and sun, which was slowly winning over the clouds. We had a nice time resting by the marker of the highest point, which Ginna climbed to be the highest walker on the wall.

The very short but tough ups and downs continued, although now more down than up. My trusted guidebook calls Hadrian's Wall "just a long walk" and perhaps the easiest of the national trails in the UK because there are no technical climbs. I read this to Anne when we were planning the journey and neglected to read a few paragraphs later about how exhausting it could be. As we approached the finish of their three-day walk, these were words repeated with some irony to me—and for some time after the trip. Somehow I got the idea that it was fairly flat overall but that had only been true of the three days before they joined me. We walked along several intense U-shaped little gaps and bowls, almost straight down and up to the next. But the weather and scenery were beautiful now, and after another hour, it was mostly downhill with longer stretches of smooth walking along well-preserved wall, no longer in the style of Clayton's Wall. We went through Caw Gap, along the Cawfield Crags, and down the path through grazing fields into Hole Gap, the final gap of the day. Oystercatchers were squawking among the cattle, and I heard curlew calls in the field as we passed fine stretches of wall and another well-preserved milecastle. Just past Hole Gap we arrived at the flooded Cawfields Quarry, where Anne, Brian, and I first saw the wall on an October morning almost two years earlier.

We rested at the car park next to the lake, used the toilets, and walked slowly to Milecastle Inn, our original destination for lunch, which had closed at 3, rather than 2:30 as the host at Beggar's Bog had said. By that point we were more tired than hungry. At least the sun was out. Our B&B was a mile and a half off the trail. A cab passed us and didn't stop when we waved at him. Anne then noticed on a signpost that the AD122 was due in ten minutes at that very spot. And in the best British manner, the bus arrived on time and picked us up. It was a "Knight Bus" ride from Harry

Potter into Haltwhistle, careening up and down hills and around steep curves into the center of the charming market town. We had a recovery pint at a perfect little British pub, the Black Bull, and more crisps, as I was getting hungry.

We called a cab to go back up the hill to our lodging, and the driver was the same guy who had charged us fifteen quid the night before to get back to Beggar's Bog from the Twice Brewed Inn. But it was only £3.50 to go to the welcoming Broomshaw Hill Farm, where Anne, Brian, and I had stayed two years before. Anne and Martin, our hosts, treated us just as well this time. We had tea and baths. I washed my clothes for the next leg and even used their clothesline. We had booked for dinner at Broomshaw, fish pie for us and pasta for Ginna—a famously picky eater—which was lovely, and collapsed soon after. I fell asleep writing my notes from the day in a warm and comfortable bed.

During these days together we passed long stretches of Clayton's Wall, with broad swaths of grass on top of the Roman stones. Clayton's Wall is beautiful. It is also fake, which is one reason I like it so much. It's not completely fake; it's built from Roman stones, and it follows the line of Hadrian's Wall correctly. But while there are many unanswered questions about Hadrian's Wall, archaeologists are certain that Clayton's Wall does not follow Roman building techniques. Hadrian's Wall had a rubble core held together by clay or mortar on a broad, deep foundation and was faced with dressed stones. Archaeologists have noted how messy parts of it are and that it might have been whitewashed and painted so in order to give it more regularity. Over the course of its 300 years of service in the Roman Empire, before the Romans withdrew from Britain, the wall was repaired and rebuilt several times because of war, neglect, and abandonment for a period of time when the frontier was moved north into present Scotland under Hadrian's successor, Antoninus. But it never looked like Clayton's Wall, with loose stone construction and a turf top, a strip of grasses running the length of the wall, about three feet wide. Not even the turf wall in the original western section of Hadrian's Wall looked like this.

Clayton rebuilt an imaginary wall that fit nineteenth-century building techniques for farms in Northumbria. It looks more like the drystone farm walls you see all over northern England, and there are more farm walls along the path than actual Hadrian's Wall. It's also quite beautiful, much narrower than Hadrian's Wall since it's penning in cattle rather than stopping Scottish barbarians charging from the wild lands to the north. You can often see Roman stones along with the field stones used in these dry stone walls, some of which must be hundreds of years old. In other words, Clayton, by all accounts a wonderfully interesting and energetic man, recreated the past in the image of his present time. And this is why I like it so much. Clayton's Wall for me is all about connections between us and the past.

We always recreate the past in the image of the present; I'm not sure we can help it. As a scholar of early Christianity, I see this over and over in how communities re-imagine Christian origins and Jesus himself. Christians today find in Jesus things that are peculiarly modern and contemporary: "Jesus is my co-pilot." "What would Jesus do?" "Buddy" Jesus? There's even a book about Jesus the salesman. Religion, like Clayton's Wall, is about our present, who and where we are today. Seeing the past as present and through the present is part of what gives religion its tremendous power to form and maintain societies. For years I have told my students that my classes are not "Bible study"; we are not reading for what the Bible means to them but for what these things meant to the people who wrote and read these stories. This is the work of history, to uncover the past and the people who lived there.

Like Clayton's Wall, the walk connects me to my past, to stories I had forgotten about my father. He was very smart, witty, often funny and even silly. He was often sarcastic with his children, traits I share, and this could produce tears when it went too far when they were younger. One of his traditions was joke names for the "from" on Christmas presents. I tried this once and Anne quickly put an end to it. He wrote clever Christmas letters years before it was the fashion. He loved music, from classical to Gilbert and Sullivan to show tunes, and took piano lessons—tickling the ivories—probably around the time he turned fifty.

He and my mother worked for Maynard Jackson, the first African-American elected mayor of Atlanta. The kids in my carpool traveling to our 95 percent white private school lamented this, claiming that every city that elected a black mayor went downhill. And yet I heard a few racist comments from my father from time to time, including rare use of the "n" word, for which I don't really blame him now. It was a racist, white context, one that a man from a small town in Illinois didn't belong to in many ways. Danville, Illinois, had plenty of racism in the '30s and '40s; it wasn't just the South, even if segregation wasn't as firmly entrenched. The man who never hunted his "dove field" was often out of his context in wealthy, traditional north Atlanta. After my father's sickness and death, I wondered how he had felt in aristocratic Atlanta among the families with generations of history there and quail farms in the south of the state.

I'm a historian because of my father and an Anglophile because of my parents, who only traveled to England overseas, except once to France when Anne and I guided them the year after we graduated from college.

That trip was at the end of our year abroad, and I finished with my parents touring Waterloo outside of Brussels after Anne had flown home to her family in Memphis. Military history was my father's passion. I also toured Gettysburg with him and one of his law school friends soon after we married, while Anne and I still lived in a small, new condo-apartment on 17th Street in DC, near Adams Morgan, the first new renovation in a neighborhood that was once largely African- and Central-American but is now completely gentrified. This was a wonderful weekend trip, memorialized by my father in one of his very clever, witty letters, written as a military dispatch from the Civil War. Somewhere in Atlanta my mother has all these letters. My father, his friend, and I toured the battlefields on a July date that was the 144th anniversary of one of the days of battle while Anne and my mother went antique shopping.

My father and his friends at Harvard Law School had formed the Gallant Pelham Club, named after John Pelham, who "was an artillery officer who served with the Confederate cavalry under J.E.B. Stuart during the American Civil War. Dubbed 'The Gallant Pelham' for his military prowess and personal courage, Pelham revolutionized the usage of light artillery as a mobile arm of the cavalry." (Yes, from Wikipedia; it's often a good source to check something you know about, which I often do before a class to make sure my memory is correct). These four young men, all married while in law school I believe, called each other Colonel to the day my father died, at least, and held wild dinner parties in Cambridge, prepared by their wives, with lots of drink and the best food they could afford. The trips to Gettysburg and Waterloo in Brussels were my father at his best: curious, energetic, witty, enjoying life and travel only five years before he killed himself.

He was an avid reader and, in the large Georgian-style house we moved into in northeast Atlanta when I was eight, shortly before my younger sisters, twins, were born and growing the family to seven, there was a library room that my parents christened "the study." It wasn't my father's office; he had an office desk in the finished basement, the first room they added air-conditioning to in maybe 1977. When I moved out after college, my room because his office. I spent many hours looking through his papers in this office, my old room, during that visit in April after he tried to commit suicide the first time. But the study was the center of his life at home. One wall was all books around a non-working fireplace. There was an old, red leather chair where he sat almost every night after he had finished the large amount of legal work he brought home—working at his desk, never in the study. He had a pitcher of "half-and-half"—a beer and a stout, the popcorn he made almost every night, and a book. If it wasn't a military history book, it would be Charles Dickens, William Thackeray, Samuel Johnson, or some other British writer from the eighteenth or nineteenth century. I think it was only at the beach that I ever saw him read a mystery, but he also always brought a history book.

Most of these books are now in the red library my mother built in the house she moved into on the northwest side of Atlanta—the "nicer" side, Buckhead—three years after his death, along with many mysteries and childhood reads such as Bobbsey Twins and Hardy Boys, from me and my sisters. There are also the older books she and her brother and sister read in the '30s and '40s such as all the Oz books and Poppy Ott, series which I also devoured in our attic in the old Atlanta house or during summers at my grandparent's farm outside of Dodgeville, Wisconsin. I took three of my father's history books with me after his funeral that sit on my shelf at home today, in this order left to right: *Battles in Britain* by William Seymour, *Gettysburg: The Second Day* by Harry Pfranz, and William Shirer's *The Collapse of the Third Republic*. Two are signed "Robert M. Royalty" in his chicken scratch writing, while *The Third Republic* is inscribed to Jerry—his father—from him, in my mother's handwriting. This book must have come back home after my grandfather died in 1974 at the age of seventy-one.

My father read English history voraciously, from the Normans to Churchill. My parents' first trip overseas was to England, when I was in sixth grade perhaps, and our first family trip was the summer after I graduated high school when my older sister was finishing eighteen months working in England. And I became an Anglophile too. I spent months in England after college, before Europe, Turkey, and Israel with Anne. I volunteered in Coventry Cathedral for the summer. Anne and I traveled during the fall until I went to Israel, where I was planning volunteer work for a few months at a Palestinian reconciliation center, the House of Hope in the Arabic city of Shef Amr in Arabic and Shefar Am in Hebrew. Three days later, my brother was killed in a car crash driven by a drunk classmate who survived. I flew home as soon as I could for weeks of terrible family grief from the calling and funeral the first week through our first Christmas without John. I visited friends in Chapel Hill, including the rector of the church I had been part of, Peter Lee, who went on to become Bishop of Virginia during the major controversy in the Episcopal Church over openly gay clergy and bishops. He told me that now I understood what grief was and would be able to reach out to others.

I remembered those words while spending a year as a student chaplain at Yale-New Haven Hospital—where Nolen was born two years later—while at Yale Divinity School. I would walk into rooms on the neurology floor, my regular assignment, as well as take call twice a month, spending the night in the Chaplain's room and hoping the pager didn't go off in the middle of the night for a death or trauma, hoping that I wouldn't have to take a family to the morgue. I wasn't well-suited for this role, and patients picked that up quickly. On the neuro floor, where patients routinely called me Father because most of them were Catholic, I sometimes got into conversations about myself and background. "I have a job as a computer programmer and operator as well, in New Haven." "A computer programmer? That's nice. I'm glad you have something to fall back on."

After my brother's sudden death and family time over Christmas to recover, I went back to London by New Year's with a work permit and didn't return to Israel for thirty years—coincidentally around John's birthday, which was, like my father's death, also in May. Anne and two college friends had a free garden flat, and she found a job in a pub while I was employed as a temp worker in the accounting office of a solicitor firm. The comptroller of the firm was from Northern Ireland, and two of my office-mates were from east London, one with a real Cockney accent. The third was a man of Caribbean background. This was without a doubt the most boring, mind-crushing job I had ever had; I literally counted the minutes until lunch, tea, and leaving. I lived in a "bedsit" flat, one room in a boarding house near Earl's Court, with a warming plate and shared bath and toilet down the hall. I had to feed coins into a meter to get electricity and pay the landlord, who smelled strongly of alcohol in the mornings, every week in cash. He lived in the garden apartment and I handed the cash through the door.

We worked until we could travel again, first with Anne's parents in England and Paris, then on to Spain, where we were robbed in Valencia. We had rented a car for the second time that year to tour the coast when we both got sick. We drove into Valencia to return the car during Las Fallas festival—yes, phallus, my never-seen object on the wall path; during the festival there were floats with large penis structures all over the city. The rental office was somewhere downtown in a maze of one-way streets, but every time I turned down a street that Anne thought would work, there was a parade coming toward us. Since I was in a feverish haze, facing brightly colored large floats—apparently for Las Fallas, size matters—marching bands, and hordes of tourists was a bit of an experience. Eventually, we stopped in a parking garage to walk to the rental office, which was closed.

When we returned to the car, all our luggage was gone from the car; fortunately, they missed our wallets and passports on the front seats. After talking to the police and driving to the airport to return the car, we stood in line at the tourist office to find a room. Two Canadian women were also in line. "Can you help us?" I cried to them. "We're really sick and all our luggage was stolen." It turned out they were sisters and one was a nurse. We got a room for one night in the same hotel they were staying in, and they gave us aspirin and a toothbrush.

At some point we both called home. Back then you had to go to a post office or telephone company and have an operator connect the call.

My father, who had converted to Roman Catholicism a few years before, said he would help in any way he could and told me to certainly use the credit card he had given me for emergencies. He added, "if all else fails, you can try the Church." I had visited enough churches that trip to know that this wasn't practical advice, and we went back to Switzerland to stay with friends I had made the summer before in Germany, a retired couple with a farmhouse next to Lake Geneva. We recovered, bought new bags and clothes, and traveled on to Italy, Croatia—still part of Yugoslavia then—and Greece. We found a cheap flight back to London through still-communist Bulgaria. On the flight from Athens to Sofia, on a Russian jetliner, we learned that non-smoking was first-come, first-served, and we ended up in the back of the plane with all the young Germans heading back from their vacations in Greece, smoking strong Turkish cigarettes. The Sofia airport was a mass of confusion and our flight to London very delayed. We kept asking the agent about our status and she continually replied, "you are not in the seestem!" Eventually, a plane arrived and we got on after pushing to the front of the gate and being crushed from behind. But we got in the front cabin along with a nice Bulgarian man with a tennis racket who said he was traveling to England to study nuclear energy. He didn't get through customs.

At the end of this trip, my parents came over and traveled with us for a week or two before my father ran in the London Marathon, seven years before he died. After the marathon, we visited a family friend I had stayed with the year before when I first arrived in England, then her brother in Kent, and some of my father's clients farther north. We then flew to Paris and drove through France for a week in the Loire Valley area and ended in Belgium. Once the marathon was behind him, it was a wonderful trip. Only six months after my brother died, the trip was restorative for all of us.

The next eight years until my father died were better for him—and for him and me—than many of the twenty-two years before, until that summer at the farm when I felt the dark clouds on the horizon.

I think about the camping trip in Wisconsin when I was young, the times my father yelled at us for not getting dressed on the weekend, the way he stuck to a rigorous routine in exercise and diet. I remember other times he yelled at me and even chased me once when I was particularly rebellious. I'm not sure he ever caught me, and he didn't beat me. But one time we all went over to the track at my new school. I must have been in seventh or eighth grade, or maybe I was in sixth grade and we knew I'd be starting there the next year. Anyway, my father had borrowed a stopwatch and wanted to do some time trials running on the track, maybe at quarter-mile intervals. I was supposed to time him, hit the button at the split time and then again for the finishing time. Somehow after he finished the mile, I hit the reset instead of the stop button so there was no time on the stopwatch. I remember bursting into tears because I was so scared of how angry he would be.

I was a precocious teen with early problems with stealing, vandalism, and drugs and alcohol in middle school, but by high school I was relatively clean and very successful. My parents went through some rough times and changes when I was in college with my mother returning to school and my father resisting her finding a new vocation as the five children grew up. The death of our brother was the biggest shock we all faced. That was 1983, and my father died in 1991. During those years, there was spiritual and emotional growth as my parents worked through their issues in therapy, and my father discovered Jungian analysis and a new spirituality as a Roman Catholic. Things changed in my early twenties and seemed different, better, around my marriage to Anne and our going to Yale for graduate school.

One might have thought my father was entering his middle life with better inner reserves, but there was also the strain of public prestige and wealth. I don't think this was necessarily his downfall, but when part of your self-image, your identity, is your wealth and possessions, and you fear they will be taken away and you'll be left with nothing because of a lawsuit, that could surely add to the spiral that leads to suicide. We hear of suicides, almost always men, when a financial scandal such as an embezzlement or pyramid scheme is exposed, or occasionally a sex scandal for a public official, although that seems rare (not the scandals, just the public shame of politicians). As far as I know there was no such scandal, only the fear of losing it all, an irrational fear that was part of his depression.

I was about twelve when my parents first bought the lot on Botany Bay Island in South Carolina and fifteen when they bought the share in the beach house where we spent that tense week the summer before he became so ill. There is no bridge to this island, so we had to leave from a marina in a shared boat, stocked with everything we needed for a few days. On one trip, my father ran into someone from Atlanta and told us about how they had compared the number of houses they owned while walking around the boats and yachts at the marina. He owned four at the time—the Atlanta home, the farmhouse and cottage at Stillwaters, and the share in the beach house. If this sounds annoying, it really was, almost disgusting—two wealthy Atlantans walking around a marina and barking about how many houses they owned.

In March, two months before he died, as we were driving to Georgia for spring break from Yale, we stopped to call from a rest area on the Georgia line, about an hour away, to update my mother on our arrival—this was long before cell phones. She told us they had sold the share in the house and wanted us to know before we got there so we wouldn't be surprised. Things were really bad by March.

A few years ago, Anne and I bought a condominium on the Cape Fear River in downtown Wilmington, North Carolina. It is a lovely spot with stunning views and a comfortable, one-bedroom place. It's nice, not overly luxurious, and we rent it out most of the time. It basically pays for itself right now with the rentals. There was immense satisfaction being there the first time and realizing this was ours. It felt great. During the first weekend there, I thought about how this made me like my father, who was obsessed at one time with owning houses. I remembered then the boasting about owning three or four houses with that other wealthy Atlantan at the marina in South Carolina. And yet all I have felt since we bought the condo is satisfaction. I know I'm not competing with my father, but there's some of him in me as well.

There are good memories of my father, but it seems there are more painful ones. Perhaps that's a legacy of death and suicide; there's no chance for any more good experiences or good memories. But those three days, walking along Clayton's Wall, walking west with my family and back into my past, were far from somber, even if they were reflective. The walk along the wall created new connections with Anne and Ginna. The center of my walk was a fun, funny, and joyous time with stories and memories we continue to share with each other. Like Clayton's Wall itself, the walk connected us through this new experience of a family trek, steep up and down hills with beautiful views, comfortable and cold rooms, good and bad meals, the "day without lunch," fantasizing about pushing a Trump supporter off a cliff, and a wild bus ride.

But Clayton's Wall is fake. It's constructed. It's manufactured to create meaning in the present according to a view of the past as present. Religion, many have argued in the sociological approach, is similarly constructed by human societies, the "sacred canopy" placed over our social world to provide meaning and prevent chaos. We build religions to build connections with each other, to make our societies function, to connect our lives to the vast universe.

Hadrian's Wall is fake in that sense, a reconstruction of the Roman wall that is a tourist destination rather than a border; there is England on both sides of the wall wherever it crops up. I was participating in a ritual of sorts, a faux ritual, perhaps, walking the wall from Wallsend to Bowness-on-Solway. I was not alone but was part of the "wall community": walkers we passed or were passed by, hikers having drinks at the Twice Brewed Inn, hosts who cater to walkers in their farmhouses and B&Bs. Ritual is part of the many social constructions of religion, just as Clayton's Wall is part of the many constructions of Hadrian's Wall, since all of it has been rebuilt at one point, either by emperors after Hadrian or by archaeologists. None of these different functions, for the wall or for religion, are bad. They just are. As a scholar of religion, I try to peel back the layers of meaning to see the different ways religion is formed and how it functions over time and within a society. In many ways I work as an archaeologist works on the wall, looking for layers, dating objects and repairs, describing the function in different times and places, trying to decide what was and what might have been, peeling back the appearances and the practices for the origins. Since I work on living religions, in particular Christianity, this often bothers people. Religion as a rule has not wanted this story told or its origins revealed. Religion tells its stories the way things "should," look, picturesque and familiar like Clayton's Wall was in the nineteenth century. Religion resists digging into its roots that reveals the flaws in its construction. Religion wants the past as a beautiful image, not a messy reality.

Historical work, like archaeology on a stone wall, can reveal the constructed nature, the fakeness of religion, just as archaeologists can show that Clayton's Wall is a fake Roman wall. And when my father saw the ways in which his religious worldview was really Clayton's Wall, his world crumbled as well. A few years before he died, my father read a book by a Catholic scholar about Jesus becoming Jesus Christ. I was in graduate school reading these types of books, but it was a new experience for him, a man who had read and retained so much history. I have never read the book and don't plan to. The scholar is not a major figure in historical studies of Jesus, and I doubt it's very good. It's painful to think about the effect of this book on my father. I know the basic argument: the Church made up just about everything of Jesus as God, especially in the fourth century after Constantine legitimated Christianity. The Church made him into a God, but he was really a man.

Those of us in the field are well aware of such arguments, although with more historical nuance. But it shook my father to his core. My mother later said he lost his faith, certainly in the Church. Jesus was a fake, or at least the Church was a fake. Clayton's Wall had been holding his faith together before the worst time of his life, and that wall collapsed. This book peeled back the beautiful turf and dry stone construction to show foundations that were not what he thought he would see. He continued to go to his Catholic church until the end of his life, when he returned to the Episcopal church. He was disciplined. But he had lost the connection. He had lost the support of a beautiful wall.

The wall, like many ancient religions, functions today as a living object. It had been reused over and over by the Romans: first, as a fortified boundary; then as a staging ground to invade the north; then as a customs border with villages around the forts; and finally, as an abandoned line of the collapsed Western Empire. An Anglo-Saxon tomb joined to the wall near Housesteads shows how the next invaders used the wall: the Roman stones found new lives in houses, churches, and many cottage and farm walls; a Roman arch and pele tower were built of Roman stones in St. Andrew's Corbridge and there's an intact Roman altar standing in St. Oswald's Heavenfield. After its rediscovery in 1600, the wall has found new life for tourists, walkers, runners, history buffs, archaeologists, and pilgrims. From Wallsend to Bowness-on-Solway, you walk past villages called Heddon-on-Wall, East Wallhouses, Walltown, Walwick, and just plain Wall; and cottages named Vallum House, Old Wall Cottage, and Low Wallhead. Today, like a religion, the wall brings new connections: connecting parks and trails across England, connecting families with nature, connecting this walker with his past.

CHAPTER 7

GREY WAGTAILS

～ Defenders

I
t was almost 8:30 in the evening and I had walked twenty miles in the previous eleven hours. Lunch seemed a long time ago, and I wasn't going to make it to my hotel that night for dinner. Give up? Miss dinner? I didn't know what to.

That morning was overcast, which matched my mood as I walked back up to the wall path, alone for the first time in three days. After a very refreshing sleep and "Full English" breakfast, including black pudding, which I love, but not Anne or Ginna, we packed up and prepared to go our separate ways again. I gave Anne some of the warmer clothes I had been carrying after checking the weather for the weekend in Carlisle and added a short-sleeved shirt she brought along for me. Even though I had been a stickler for carrying all my clothes and gear, having their suitcases delivered to our lodgings three days in a row was pretty convenient. Our host Martin drove Anne and Ginna to the station in Haltwhistle to head back to London while I walked out down the driveway of Broomshaw Hill, crossed the lane, and found the trail along Haltwhistle Burn back up to Cawfields Quarry, where we had caught the AD122 bus the day before.

The path led uphill through the woods along the rocky creek with cliffs along the other side. After spying a couple of new birds, a siskin and a grey wagtail, I walked slowly, eyeing the brush and low branches. After crossing Haltwhistle Burn on a small footbridge, I emerged into a cleared area with abandoned old brick works and the remnants of a ruined farmhouse. A short stretch along the B6318 took me past the Milecastle Inn again, which was still closed. I'm not sure it's ever open and probably doesn't even serve lunch.

I followed the road to the quarry carpark, my third visit and second in two days, took a comfort break at the public loo, then took off west again on the wall path. I had already walked one-and-three-quarters miles, uphill with an elevation gain of already 150 feet. I would regret not catching a ride back to Cawfields instead of walking on my own uphill from Broomshaw Hill.

Less than a mile from the quarry is Great Chesters, the Roman fort of Aesica. It was great indeed, partially excavated and full of lumpy green mounds with Roman stone peeking out and evocative bits of wall revealing the corners of the fort. I walked slowly around the entire fort before stopping to leave a two-pence coin among the pile of coins on the Roman altar, the only altar still *in situ* along the path—that is, standing where it was found rather than being moved to a museum.

I walked on past a farm gate that had re-used a Roman milestone as a post and then along bits of wall in between lots of drystone farm walls. At my guidebook's suggestion, I turned to look east for a fine view of the crags from the day before. It was indeed a stunning view against the morning clouds and reminded me how hard the ups and downs had been. Ahead, there was one more crag yet to cross. After passing through a small copse of trees, I started climbing again toward Walltown Crag. A farmer with two border collies; one in training on a long lead went by in front of me, herding a small flock of maybe ten sheep. They ignored me as I stopped to watch and take pictures. He was yelling at the dog, to my ears at least, but that was probably just part of the training, giving firm and sharp commands.

Walltown Crag did not disappoint. It was a nice climb past the romantically named King Arthur's Turret, up to one of the best stretches of wall I had seen on the entire walk so far. The wall, here unrestored in large stretches, often followed entire swags of undulating hills, which were gentler than the steep U-shaped hills and passes we had negotiated with some difficulty on the previous "day without lunch." There were stunning views in all directions. My pace was faster as well and my spirits lifted after the slightly gloomy departure that morning. In the midst of the Crag was one of the best-preserved turrets on the path as well as one of the highest stretches of wall. A couple of walkers passed me going the other direction, but I was alone for almost the entire time along the last big hill heading west, according to my guidebook.

I walked down the last of Walltown Crag past another quarry pond, Walltown Quarry, now in Walltown County Park, which includes both Walltown Lodge and, yes, Walltown Refreshments. In England, when a name works, they just keep using it. This was where I stopped for a break and snack before returning to the trail. There were a lot of people in the park, enjoying the warmer weather on the Saturday of a bank holiday weekend, the British equivalent of Memorial Day weekend but with no special history that I'm aware of. As I walked out the parking lot to the road, I snapped a picture of the departing AD122 as a memento of the wild ride the day before—I did not get a look at the driver, The path was relatively flat after the hills of the morning, which was good because my right knee had started to hurt again. I had been wearing the brace the entire walk as a precaution, which probably got me through most of the crags, but on day seven the knee made its presence known once again. I was not happy about that with three days ahead of me.

While there were only short bits of wall along this section after leaving the Walltowns, there was a lot of Roman ditch and vallum again, which I hadn't seen for a few days. I passed the ruins of Thirwall ("gap in the wall") Castle, built from Hadrian's Wall stone, and headed along the path next to a long stretch of ditch, some of which was flooded, with vallum to the south. A charity walk for cancer was walking the other direction, from Gilsland to Walltown Park, and I passed many walkers of all ages with bright blue t-shirts.

I passed Greenhead, one lunch option a bit farther from the path, but I kept on. I made it to Gilsland for lunch before 2 p.m., which was the earliest lunch I had to that point of solo hiking. The trail through Gilsland wound around behind buildings and through people's gardens. I was supposed to cross the railroad tracks to a field to find the well-preserved Poltross Burn Milecastle, but there was construction and a diversion on the path. One of the features I missed here, according to my guidebook, along with barracks and an oven, are stairs that allow archaeologists to estimate the height of the walkway on the wall, at twelve feet.

I had a sandwich at a tea shop, the House of Meg, after a character in Sir Walter Scott's *Waverly*, which also inspired the murals on the walls. I took my time, resting and charging my phone. On the way out, I crossed a cracked bridge on the other side of the field to see if I could get back to the Poltross Burn Milecastle, but there was no access across the railway tracks. As I headed off, I found myself in Cumbria and had walked over eight miles. I thought I was doing well. I was wrong.

The day had turned brighter and much warmer. On my way out of

Gilsland, I saw the dilapidated house, once an inn actually built into the wall itself, when the diversion for the railroad rejoined the path. The next hour to the Roman fort of Birdoswald brought some of the best stretches of wall along the walk—and the last, because that afternoon I would see the last remaining wall in Cumbria. One long stretch just out of Gilsland revealed a view of two well-preserved turrets at once, spaced one-third of a Roman mile apart. Stairs led down to the River Irthing, passing Willowford Farm, which had faux Roman plaques on one of the farmhouse walls for walkers to see. Here I saw the large abutments of the Roman Willowford Bridge across the Irthing, now maybe 500 feet from the river, showing how much its course had changed over 1800 years. This crossing marked the end of the original stone wall and the beginning of the turf wall leading to the coast. This was also the end of narrow wall on broad wall foundations; when the Romans converted the turf wall to stone, they built foundations that matched the width of the wall.

After crossing the beautiful and strikingly modern steel Irthing Bridge, the path made a sharp turn and went up a steep hill. A couple walking with their dog and I had been more or less together for thirty minutes and continued to Birdoswald together. At the top of the hill was Milecastle 49 and then the longest stretch of wall surviving today. My guidebook told me there were engravings along here, including a large phallic symbol. The author Henry Stedman, a man I felt I knew pretty well by this point, gave specific instructions to find this near a culvert in the wall as I approached Birdoswald, but I could not find any markings at all. So far I was 0-3 when it came to Roman phalluses.

A few minutes later I walked into the fort, called Banna ("spur") by the Romans since it sits on a spur of land over the river, to find a huge kite festival. Flags were flying, and children and families were playing with kites. It wasn't a good time to get pictures of Roman ruins. The excavations are behind a stone farmhouse and farm building, now owned by English Heritage, with shops and tearoom and toilets. The farmyard had picnic tables where I could sit a bit and leave my pack to use the toilet. I had a snack, got my passport stamped in the shop—number 5! 2 to go!—and headed west into the fields with a large run of vallum to my left.

There were also undulations in the ground from the turf wall as I crossed in and out of fields, at one point directed around three fields to avoid another bull. Perhaps the Cumbrian authorities or farmers are more focused on protecting walkers. Runners passed me heading east, and a shouted question to one of the them told me they planned to complete the entire route in three days. "Good luck!" I shouted back. "I'll need it!" he answered. Thinking back to the crags and my right knee, I thought, *Yes, you will.*

After this patch of large cattle fields along the Birdoswald spur, I walked on through a more rolling countryside of smaller fields with sheep and woods, crossing streams with names such as Wall Burn, Sandy Sike, and Pipers Sike as I headed toward Banks, about an hour from Birdoswald. That hour was another three-and-a-half miles. I climbed another ridge to a series of turrets and a Roman signal tower built before the wall, probably for Agricola's campaign into Scotland, which was then incorporated into the wall by a bend in its construction. The views were now to the south, suggesting the theory that the Romans were more worried about the Britons on the southern side than the northern side.

I enjoyed the ruins and the views, including the only good shot of the walk of a black sheep in a field of white ones, but it was getting late on a hot day, and I was running low on water. For some reason I did not refill enough at Birdoswald, so I was counting on Banks to fill up my bottle, where I also hoped to visit Lanercost Priory, built in 1166 out of stone from the wall. It was after 5 p.m. when I arrived at Banks up the hill, where I found no water, no shop, no tea room, nobody at all. The Priory was to close at 6, and I was starting to get worried about the distance to my lodging before the kitchen closed. Time was no longer on my side, and there had been a lot more hills to negotiate than I had hoped for. Even though the general course of the trail was down toward the sea, the land continued to roll up and down on this gradual decline.

Just down the hill from Banks I saw the last bit of Roman wall in Cumbria, according to my guidebook, a short section with a high piece that was built in the nineteenth century from Roman stones—hence the height. Once again there was a Roman inscription on the back, from a stone taken from a site farther west called—and I'm not making this up—Moneyholes. But I couldn't find it, so I was 0-4 on finding little Roman extras on the big wall. There wasn't much light at this time in the late afternoon.

I crossed a small road at Haytongate and found no drinks in the "honesty" snack box for walkers, nor a public toilet. Then, crossing another stream, this one Bartholme Beck—I cannot explain the differences among a burn, a sike, and a beck—I saw the last piece of wall at this end of the path, not much wall at all, really, but quite evocative of the state of the wall before reconstruction. Roman stones were mostly covered with grass, shrubs, and even a tree stump. A sharp barb-wired fence, marking a boundary between two fields, kept walkers away. I trudged on to Walton, which was actually down in a valley, listening to the faint slosh of the half-inch of water left in my bottle. It was warm and I was thirsty.

Crossing a tributary of the River Irving on Dovecote Bridge, I looked in vain for the remnants of a Roman bridge abutment to my right and headed on the road through a small field. Just as I walked into Walton, I was delighted to find a young couple and a small child playing in the front garden of a house. There was a barn to the right and a couple of picnic tables. The couple had just opened a bunkhouse for walkers, Florrie's, and very kindly refilled my water bottle. They said I was welcome to stay and we chatted a bit as I stretched my sore right knee and studied the route. I should have taken a picture, they were so nice, but all of a sudden I saw that I had six miles to Crosby-on-Eden, and it was already 7 p.m. Dinner was looking unlikely. I panicked, jumped up, put my pack on, and said goodbye and thank you very quickly. I started to walk while reading the guidebook, and I saw that Park Broom Lodge, my room for the night, was thirty minutes outside Crosby. OK, maybe less than five miles, but I picked up the pace for the next mile and a half into Newtown, averaging under twenty minutes a mile. I was dashing through different farms, driveways, car parks, and the backs of gardens at what was for me breakneck speed. As I walked into Newtown, I kept walking past the village green on the improbably named Via Verdi toward where the path branched off again to the left, not sure at all what to do.

Bend, don't break. I stopped and sat down and took a breath in the park. Finally, I pulled out the guidebook and noticed that Park Broom Lodge would pick guests up in Carlisle by prior arrangement. I called the lodge, told them my plight, and as it turned out Bill, the husband of Kath, the proprietor, was out picking up someone else up and could come get me in Newtown in maybe thirty or forty-five minutes. I sat and waited and rested on a bench in the green after turning off my hike tracker on my phone at 19.67 miles. A hard day, a long and hot afternoon, and I was very tired. This was the second time I had badly estimated the total distance to my lodging by counting to the town rather than the actual place, and I was very frustrated with myself. Another low point. I wasn't bushwhacking through the Serengeti; I was walking across the most settled country in the world with a clear path, a detailed guidebook, and Google Maps, for crying out loud. Time to beat myself up a little while waiting for the ride.

About an hour later I was at the lodge after a ride with a German couple and the kind owner. I checked in, ordered a beer and my meal since the kitchen was closing soon, and ran upstairs for a shower and change before dinner. Feeling refreshed and in rising spirits again, I took my guidebook and iPad to the dining room with the plan to reconsider tomorrow and the final day. But two tables down were Shirley and Alice, and their conversation provided the entertainment for some time. Shirley, I learned, was a retired midwife, a widow whose husband had been in the Royal Navy, and maybe the cutest old lady I've ever seen. She looked to be in her nineties, but I learned later that she was only in her seventies. She was bent over with maybe arthritis but clearly still going strong. She talked about rationing sweets as a child and that she couldn't make toffee until she was fourteen. After a while I stopped pretending to read my guidebook and started taking notes: "If we're around next Christmas!" "If he's plugged he's plugged, there's nothing you can do about it." "We were never sure if it was romantic or not. He used to go by and light the fire for her each day." "They dug the hole on top of him and put the dog in when he died. What are they going to do when she dies?" "My father died on a bank holiday. They had to hold his body over until Tuesday." "I wanted to grow old gracefully, but I'm growing old without grace." But she had plenty of grace, I snuck one picture from my table. After a nightcap in the lounge, where there was internet, I went up for a good night's sleep.

The next morning I ate and packed and then waited for a ride back to Newtown. Bill dropped me off at the exact spot where I had called the night before. I was happy not to miss an inch of the path after all and started off before 10 a.m. It was fine weather and would turn quite warm by the afternoon. The miles to Carlisle were smooth and fast and pleasant; blessedly, there were no real hills all day. There were no Roman artifacts either in the pleasant countryside except stretches of ditch and vallum. Shortly, I passed the Carlisle airport, which we had driven past the night before on my way to the lodge, and, more charming, Bleatarn (Blue Tarn) Farm, site of a Roman quarry for the wall, but now a tarn or lake, hence the name. Mounds covering the base of unexcavated wall could still be seen. Just past Bleatarn was another honesty box with a sign:

The Stall-on-the-Wall
Please Pay Using the Honesty Box . . .
By Decree of the Emperor Hadrian

There was a picture of Hadrian and an advert for the Bleatarn Holiday Cottages. Underneath the picture of Hadrian was the ubiquitous, but incongruous, blue thumbs-up symbol and "Like us on Facebook." I stopped here and chatted briefly with some walkers, including a father and his pre-teen son who had started early that morning at the terminus in Bowness-on-Solway.

It took me two hours to get to the turn-off to Park Broom Lodge that I had been heading for the evening before. I was thankful I had shifted those miles from Saturday to Sunday, which was originally supposed to be a shorter day; I would have been very tired and hungry if I hadn't stopped and called for a ride. The two-day total would be the same in any case. Since Park Broom Lodge was so far past Crosby-on-Eden, part of the day's "extra" was really scheduled for today all along since I had originally counted miles from Crosby in my planning. My planning of distances and difficulty for the walk was, overall, lousy. But now I had to keep moving.

Leaving the course of the wall itself, the path followed the bends of the River Eden all the way toward Carlisle. It was very flat now. I saw a huge flock of gulls in a field there, probably the most I had ever seen. Soon, I joined a road that crossed the busy M6 on an overpass. I had been walking through neighborhoods of detached houses in Linstock when I reached the overpass, where two Dutch walkers were resting on their way into Carlisle for the night. We chatted a bit before I headed on. The path left the road and continued on a lovely suburban cycleway into Rickerby Park, which includes the Victorian village of Rickerby, complete with a tower folly on the right. I followed a path in the park toward the river.

And this is where the day started to go wrong. The directions in my guidebook were vague, and I didn't read the map well at all. I continued following what I thought was the path to the Spenny Bridge across the River Eden, but I went east, to the right, when I was supposed to bear left. I ended up walking a big loop around the park, about a mile, until I saw that the bridge I was walking toward was the A7 bridge for cars and trains with no access from the park. I finally stumbled onto a trail along the river and followed it another half-mile back upstream until I came to the iron Spenny Bridge. This was a Sunday of the bank holiday weekend, warm and sunny, and the park was full of families, runners, and cookouts. As I finally crossed the footbridge, after taking a sour-faced selfie, I saw the Dutch pair ahead of me. The path on the other side of the river branched into two, and I followed them until I realized they were going into Carlisle. I turned around, but this second wrong turn of the morning added another half-mile.

Back on the correct path along the south bank of the Eden, I walked past a school and golf course to the Sands Sports Centre. Just in front of the center is an artistic replica of the entirety of Hadrian's Wall. The "wall" is about two feet high, three courses of bricks, interrupted by stone rectangular "towers" with marble tops engraved with the names of all the Roman forts. I had one of the earlier lunches of the walk at the Centre Café. I took my time, got my penultimate passport stamp, and remembering that my bed and breakfast that night did not take a credit card, looked around for a cash machine. The center had bathrooms but no ATM, so I walked about a half-mile into the city center to find one in a shopping center. This involved a lot of subways or underground passes in a busy intersection, walking past the Ristorante Italiano Adriano, although the sign actually read RIST RANTE ITALIANO A RIANO. I returned to the Sands Center to rejoin the path along the Eden. I had turned off my route tracker but it was almost a mile roundtrip, with my pack, on the hot pavement of Carlisle to get the cash.

This path led through a large city park, Bitts Park, full of tennis courts, playgrounds, small gardens, lots of families, and the Carlisle Cricket Club on the other side of the river. As I walked along, I saw, but ignored, a diversion sign for the path. Leaving the park, I headed for the bridge over the River Caldew, which joined the Eden here, but the bridge was closed for construction. The diversion! Surely I can get around somehow, I thought, so I turned left to follow the Caldew to find another place to cross. I followed a drive around the edge of the park for about a quarter-mile until I reached the railroad tracks. There was no possibility of climbing over the embankment and crossing the tracks leading into Carlisle Station, so I continued around the edge of the park almost all the way back to the Sands Center, to the previously ignored signpost where the diversion was marked in bright red arrows on a map of Carlisle. You Are Here in a large red word-balloon pointed to my spot. I stared at the map for a while with a sinking feeling. I had walked a mile in a circle from this very spot. The red arrow on the map was taunting me. And the path ahead back to Hadrian's Wall Path through the city center looked long and tricky.

I took a picture of the map and headed back out of the park on a different path, almost due south instead of northwest, where the closed bridge across the River Caldew lay. This led back to the busy roundabout I had already negotiated for the ATM. This time I turned right into a different subway—one of about eight—heading toward Castle Way, a busy four-lane ring road with parallel side streets. I only walked about five minutes up the hill to Carlisle Castle, an imposing structure dating from Henry I in the twelfth century, when I realized this was not going to work. It was 3:30 in the afternoon. I had been pounding pavement in a series of wrong turns and diversions for three hours. I had walked almost thirteen miles already. I was tired, it was hot, and my feet were starting to hurt along with my sore right knee.

It was time again to bend and not break. I walked down another subway under the road to the Tullie Museum. There, I found a very friendly chap, Graham, sweeping up broken beer bottles outside the museum entrance; the subways of Carlisle must be quite the scene overnight. I asked him about finding a cab, and he very kindly said he would call one for me. I used their loo and, after thanking Graham again and snapping a photo of him, perched myself out on the side street, finally taking my pack off. Shortly, a car pulled up, and I put my pack in the boot and showed the driver the photo of the diversion in the wall path. He peered at my photo for a minute or so and said, "I think I know where this is." And sure enough, maybe ten minutes later, he dropped me at the corner of Harvey Street and Engine Lonning, the endpoint of the diversion. Much relieved, I followed the path that led to the river, where I rejoined Hadrian's Wall Path. That was the best five pounds I spent the entire walk and the smartest move of what was turning out to be a longer, hotter day than planned.

Optimism returned as I left Carlisle. And, indeed, I was making decent time and would be at Hillside Farm in good order. I was determined today not to miss out on dinner and maybe get a shower before dinner, so I set a blazing pace relative to even the day before. But the afternoon was quite warm, and my feet were starting to hurt badly. The path followed the river for a bit over a mile then cut off to the west through farm fields to rejoin the line of the wall after the long loop through Carlisle and its suburbs. I paused at St. Mary's Beaumont, the only church on the line of the wall itself, built on a hill with a view of the countryside; hence, *Beaumont*, "beautiful view" in Norman French. Originally on this spot, there was a Norman motte-and-bailey, a small castle on the mound with a courtyard below. I made a wrong turn leaving Beaumont, only about four minutes down the wrong road, but I rued the time. By now my feet were killing me. They were on fire.

The path followed a gentle downward slope from Beaumont as I neared the Firth of Solway, which flows into the Irish Sea. I was really wearing down as I went on through the village of Burgh-by-Sands, site of a Roman fort, and the final leg to Bousted Hill about two miles farther, just grinding out the last few miles. I walked up to my B&B at 6:35, another fine time, for about eight-and-a-half hours total walking for the twenty-and-one-half miles. I was sweaty and exhausted.

Hillside Farm is a handsome brick Grade II listed building and working farm in the tiny horsey hamlet of Bousted Hill, overlooking the sandy scrub of Burgh Marsh and the River Eden, which flows into the Firth. Sandra, my host, greeted me along with her three-year-old granddaughter Hope. I checked in and went upstairs, the only guest for the night, almost stumbling into the room. My last room for the walk was a high-ceilinged, large room with fine views across the marsh. Hope had the bath before me. I peeled off my shoes and discovered some bad chafing and really large blisters—actually, not large, huge. I had just pushed too far too fast and was wearing the wounds. The route mapping program has a graph for each day, with red for elevation and blue for speed. Whereas usually the speed varies a lot, up and down, the blue line graph for this day was flat and fast. I had booked it.

Wincing at all the new pains from the day, I undressed, bathed, then dressed and washed a shirt one last time for tomorrow, hanging it outside on the clothesline in the courtyard behind the house and next to the stables. Everything was hurting. Sandra drove me back to the pub at Burgh-by-Sands—pronounced "Bruff," I learned in the car—and told me to tell anyone at the bar to call her when I was ready to be picked up, quite a change from the mean host at Beggar's Bog who dropped us and left us to face a long wait for a fifteen-pound cab ride. I could barely walk back and forth from my table to order at the bar from the pains in blisters and knee, but settled in for a pint and a meat pie with chips and peas. Rested but still sore after an hour or so at my table, I asked the young woman at the bar to call for me, and Sandra soon arrived to pick me up as promised. She was very curious about the quality of my meal on the way back, probably because her bed-and-breakfast business depended on guests enjoying this pub. Like many Brits, she is insistent on a full-crust pie, and I reported that it was that, authentic and very satisfying indeed. ·

I walked slowly, painfully slowly, up to my beautiful room and watched the sunset over the Firth.

Embodiment is a word tossed around a lot in the study of religion. We study beliefs, ideas about God, and the grand history of traditions, sometimes forgetting that we are talking about actual people who have aches and pains, families to worry about, and dreams of their own. I didn't have that problem on the walk. Walking for nine days with a pack at age fifty-five is a good way to get in touch with one's embodiment. This started with the injury to my right knee in April, the same week I took the body blow at work of being passed over yet again. I wore a brace the whole time for support, although it also was a reminder of my physical frailty. By day eight, I was in a lot of pain. The knee started hurting in earnest once I left the hills and my family at Great Chesters on day seven. I then had to push very hard the next two days, almost twenty miles each, developing severe, full-heel blisters the size of quarters on day eight that made the normal blisters on day three look pretty good. I also had hot shooting pains and numbness down my left leg and feet during most of the walk, which I thought at the time was muscle strain but learned from my physical therapist once back at home that they were from the L4 and L5 vertebrae pushing on spinal nerves. Recovery took another steroid shot in the knee and another three months of physical therapy for the knee and back. It wasn't until July that I started getting back over fifty miles a week on my road bike.

In the last twelve years or so, I've had maybe fifteen steroid injections in my shoulder, neck, hands, and now knee, and I've been in physical therapy pretty regularly for the past eight years. When I turned fifty and was having terrible lower back spasms, neck pain from stenosis, and eventually rotator cuff surgery, my doctor was kind enough to point out that I had fallen apart. She left family practice a year or two later to teach geriatric medicine at a major hospital; I'm not sure if I had anything to do with that. None of these aches and pains are unusual for an active fifty-five-year-old who keeps attempting 100-mile bike rides and nine-day hikes. These have been hindrances but, so far, not obstacles.

And I discovered that, on a long walk such as this, life becomes simplified, focused, and clear. Everything I had went in my backpack each morning. The only task I had besides walking to the next inn or bed and breakfast was to enjoy the day: the history, the scenery, and the birds. In other words, the goal was to enjoy the moment as the miles ticked by. Yes, I did look at the time and think about how long it was to lunch or arrival at my room for the night, sometimes in a mild panic. I walked and looked, spied some birds, and I thought. For nine days, I carried everything I had. And I had to keep going. I suppose that's true in a sense of any travel, but on mile ten out of twenty for the day, the only way to go was forward. This wasn't a day trip. I didn't have a car. I couldn't turn back to the inn I had checked out of that morning. I had to keep going.

But I faced obstacles from the very first day to this blistery penultimate walk to Bousted Hill, way back to Newcastle, when I avoided being mugged by a gang of ten-year-old boys. You've walked these with me so far: the missed diversion on the trail on day one that led me through and around a construction site on the River Tyne; the wrong turn toward Aydon Castle that added an hour on the way to Corbridge; dancing around the bull while approaching Acomb; calling my hotel on day seven and moving those miles to the next day; and calling a cab in Carlisle rather than slogging the hard sidewalks with sore blisters, a throbbing right knee, and shooting pains down my left leg.

These diversions, minor as they might sound, upset my plan. I wasn't supposed to stop in Newtown that night or take a cab through Carlisle. But a lesson from twenty-five years ago—bend, don't break— ran through my mind. So I changed my plan.

I felt like I had to keep going. As I thought about this during the walk, sort of "meta-thinking" about what was happening, I thought about how we live this way every day. It sounds trite, I'm sure, to say that we have to keep going, and perhaps it is trite. But think about how hard that can be. We all have lived in the past, dwelling on successes or failures or resentments, rather than moving ahead. And we have all known someone who couldn't move forward. We say they are paralyzed—by grief, fear, indecision, depression. They can't "get on with their lives." They can't move. The metaphor of movement, of progress along our life's journey or pilgrimage is fundamental to how we think about ourselves and our lives. There are many paths, yes, but only one direction—forward.

Hadrian could not move forward after Antinous's death. We know about Antinous because of Hadrian's public, powerful grief that obsessed him for the rest of his life. There are at least 100 marble images of Antinous discovered so far, more than any other ancient Roman besides Augustus and Hadrian himself. Hadrian immediately deified Antinous—against convention, since this was still reserved for the senate—and built a temple-tomb to his dead lover in a new city across the Nile. His magnificent villa outside Rome included a temple to Antinous and multiple statues and images of his beloved. I visited this villa the December after the walk. The Antinoeion, as the temple was called, is only a ruin now, but huge—a football-field-sized temple complex. The cult begun by Hadrian in 132 continued long enough to be critiqued by Christians in the fourth century, for whom Antinous was seen as a rival savior to Christ. If Hadrian loved Antinous during his life as fiercely as he grieved and memorialized him after his death, then it was a powerful infatuation indeed.

Maybe it gets harder to move on. I am not sure we look back more as we grow older, but there is more to look back on: regrets, resentments, joys, successes. We carry the past with us, just as I carried my pack forward every day. Sometimes that feels very heavy indeed, sometimes lighter, but we carry who we are. The pack gets heavier as we get older, as dreams fade or become realities, as we lose loved ones. This burden, the things he carried, must have been very heavy for my father. And he could not keep going.

I won't ever know exactly what was going on the year or so before he killed himself. Something went wrong in my father's world, in his head, and he couldn't get over it. He couldn't move on. He couldn't bend. I think about the camping trip in Wisconsin, the times he yelled at us for not getting dressed on the weekend until late in the morning, the way he stuck to a rigorous routine in exercise and diet. He was very disciplined and never very flexible. When the blow of the lawsuit fell, he was not able to bend. It stayed in his head and surely contributed to a disease that might have taken its toll regardless, but might not have led to suicide. We all carry burdens in our heads. I'll never know what other burdens he was carrying along his path.

After twenty-five years, I told the story of his death in public for the first time. And still I wonder what might have been different.

CHAPTER 8

MEW GULLS

🦅 Rescuers

After 106 miles, you would think the last six miles would be a cakewalk, and I'd be full of confidence. You would be wrong.

Exhausted, I slept well in that lovely high-ceilinged old room. But I struggled even to get dressed for breakfast, which was served downstairs in the large dining room with a northern window and a view of the marsh and river. I was stiff and sore, chafed, and my feet were painfully tender. Don't ask me how I got down the stairs because I don't know. As soon as I sat, alone in the dining room, I wondered if I'd be able to walk back upstairs, put on my boots, and hoist my pack one last time. Coffee wasn't strong enough that morning, but that's all I had; Sandra didn't stock rocket fuel. The customary food photos are a bit blurry, so I suppose my hands were a little shaky.

Once photographed, I ate my last "Full English" of the walk, paid Sandra in cash, and crawled back upstairs—OK not literally, not on my hands and knees—to pack one more time. She was grateful for my extra excursion in downtown Carlisle the day before, pounding the pavement, with the pack, to get the pounds. I bid her a fond farewell after a selfie on the front porch. I walked slowly down her stairs and back down the short hill—Bousted Hill, typical descriptive English place name—to the wall path. It lay on the south side of the road, along a dike. I paused here at an old black-and-white iron signpost with Bousted Hill in a circle at the top:

Bousted Hill ¼ (pointing back behind me)
Burgh by Sands 2¼, Carlisle 11¼ (pointing to my right)
Port Carlisle 4½, Bowness 5½

Behind this a newer brown sign with white letters:

Exercising of Horses on Marsh is Prohibited

A typical English sign; I found they are much fonder of rules, rotas, and such in England than we are in America. And finally a larger, foreboding sign:

Road Liable to Flooding.

But the tide was low, and there was no rain in sight.

The Victorian-looking signpost pointed to the edge of Bowness, not the trail head, as indicated in my guidebook. I had about six and a half miles to go that morning, with a train reservation in Carlisle that afternoon. I really wasn't sure I would make it to Bowness, let alone make my train. Since this was a Monday bank holiday, with limited train service, that would be a big problem. Fortunately, the path was mostly flat today as it followed the River Eden out to the Firth of Solway. Still, it took a quarter of a mile—almost ten minutes!—to get up to a decent walking speed. As my athletic trainer says, "motion is lotion." Somehow the joints unstuck and I could move. There were a few walkers and horse folk heading the other direction, so I tried to look stalwart and sure on my feet. Once I was able to ignore the blister pain on my feet, I was able to keep that pace most of the way.

I had to negotiate a couple of horse fences along the first mile or so, which meant stopping and restarting. Momentum was on my side—I could bend forward a bit and the pack carried me along, sort of—so every start and restart was reliving the morning pain. I felt like an old, old car in cold weather. Soon I had a friend, a little black-faced lamb who found himself on the path side of the road while the main flock was across in the field. There was a high hedge to the left, so he scampered ahead of me on the path as well. Eventually, two other sheep joined him and led him back across the road to the fields along the River Eden. In the distance I could see, across Burgh Marsh, the channel of the River Esk. When they joined, they would become the Firth of Solway at Port Carlisle, just a mile and a half from Bowness.

At the hamlet of Drumburgh—I suppose "Drum-bruff" but no one was around to ask—the path veered south away from the firth and open dike. I followed a road and crossed some fields, one of which had a kissing gate to pass through but no fence on either side. To "fulfill all righteousness"—Matthew 3:15, I thought to myself—I used the gate properly rather than go around it and continued through the next field, where there was in fact a fence penning a group of maybe six or eight young holsteins. It must have been feeding time because they seemed awfully glad to see a person and crowded around me, but I had to move on. I followed roads and went through some woods and farms. The details are a little hazy about most of that morning—I was not at my best—but at some point the Dutch walkers from Carlisle passed me. After leading me astray when we crossed the river together on the footbridge the day before, they had walked into the city for lunch and spent the night. So they had come from Carlisle that morning with about ten or twelve miles already done. They were traveling light with daypacks, so maybe they had a luggage delivery service. They were spending the night in Bowness. They were quite chipper compared to me. If Dutch people yodel, they would have been yodeling. They moved on while I struggled behind and soon lost sight of them.

Approaching the village of Glasson, the wall path zigged north along some painful paved road then zagged back left to follow the firth westward. This section was in woods again with intermittent views of the firth off to the right. There was a short climb, very hard at this point, and then flat into Port Carlisle, where the views opened wide to the glorious firth. Small hillocks of tufty grass ran to little drop-offs and furrows, sort of like the bunkers in Scottish links golf courses but not as sheer or high. Beyond that, wide expanses of marshy beach with shiny tidal pools and tufts of grasses ran all the way to the water, which must have been a half-mile away. Port Carlisle has not been a port since 1853 when the canal closed, and ruined hulks and structures were still visible along the strand. From firth-side there didn't seem to be a lot going on in the village. I passed a Methodist chapel and the back of a pub. Most importantly, I passed two cheery and enterprising gents sitting along the path to greet walkers in front of a shed that adjoined Niall's house. Niall had a white beard and nautical look. His mate, Ian, was a good bit bulkier, clean-shaven and bald, with black shorts revealing white, thick legs above black socks and boots. When he noticed my knee brace, and I told him it was quite sore now, he gleefully showed me the long scar on his left knee from his surgery the month before.

Niall was in charge. This was his house and his business for walkers. There was a ten- or twelve-foot sign post with white paint and black lettering. At the top, a circular sign read Port Carlisle 2016. Underneath, in case anyone walking by was confused about where they were, a rectangular sign proclaimed in all-caps, HADRIAN'S WALL. Beneath were two finger posts, one pointing east: WALLSEND 83, and the other due west: BOWNESS ON SOLWAY 1. For a pound, he would put your hometown and a couple other cities on the post and take your picture.

I was too tired to figure out how far Indianapolis was, but Niall was ready with Chicago, so I told him to subtract 100 miles from Chicago and put it up there. He assembled the letters: INDIANAPOLIS 4058, pointing west and slightly south. For some reason he put Durham, England, on there as well, clocking in at 102 miles. Underneath the Wallsend sign post, he quickly added 30 MAY AM, so we would remember the date, if not the precise time. Along the post itself, going straight down, read THANK YOU with the money box below. And then he took several pictures on my phone of a grinning Bob, holding his hiking poles tightly. I grabbed a shot of Niall pointing proudly at his sign and then the pair in their chairs before heading off.

This was the end of walking path. I finished on the road into Bowness, which unfortunately went uphill about fifty-six feet over a half mile before starting a gentle slope to the hut that marks the end, or beginning for some, of Hadrian's Wall Path. I stopped for several selfies at the village sign and the final fingerpost marking 130 yards to the finish and 260 yards to the public facility—indicated with the letters WC for water closet—in the village. Then a right turn off the High Street into an alley, a left along a small garden path, and I was there. I had finished!

And I really needed to pee.

There was no way I could make it another 130 yards, and I didn't want to leave the hut without celebrating my accomplishment. Luckily, there was no one around, and I found a bit of shelter on the lee side of the wall.

Then I sat back down and observed my surroundings while I started to savor the moment. It really was just a small, open-aired hut with a large opening to the firth. There were Latin signs above the two entrances for walkers finishing and starting. Above the door I had passed through, there was a wooden sign with red lettering that read, under a picture of Hadrian:

WELCOME
THE END OF HADRIAN'S WALL PATH
AVE TERMINUM CALLIS HADRIANI AUGUSTI PERVENISTI

The Latin reads: Welcome to those who have reached the end of Hadrian Augustus's path.

On the other side, a similar sign reads:

WALLSEND 84 MILES; GOOD LUCK GO WITH YOU

This was then translated into Latin:

SEGENDUNUM MP LXXXIV : FORTUNA VOBIS ADSIT

The floor was decorated with a large tile mosaic, faux Roman style, facing the bench with AVE MAIA, welcome walkers, on both sides.

I was very happy. I sat down next to the stamp box to prepare for the final stamp, the moment of glory, all alone. I was sitting in the small hut that marks the western end, relishing the end of the trek while preparing to stamp my wall passport at the final station.

And then the family showed up.

The bank holiday was a bright, blustery and cool day, in other words, perfect seaside weather in England. I had walked all day in my athletic wicking t-shirt and long sleeve hiking shirt without getting warm—granted I was walking painfully slowly. In northern England, sunny and the mid 50s clearly means "beach!" Or, "seaside!" as they say there. There were four, two pre-teen girls and their parents, all dressed as only the British can for the beach. The father was wearing tight shorts and a tank top revealing acres of reddish, freckly white skin. The older of the girls exclaimed loudly, on seeing the sign above the western door for walkers just starting out, "Hadrian! I thought his name was Adrian!" The younger sister came in the hut, sat down, and began stamping her arm with the stamp in the passport box, which felt sacrilegious to me. I hadn't stamped mine yet! Her left arm was soon covered with black circles containing profiles of Hadrian with "The Banks" underneath. Peering over the ledge down to the sandy shoals, I could see why they had chosen this name.

I decided to take advantage of this interruption to my moment of triumph and asked if they would take a picture of me here at the end of the trail. The mother immediately said to her husband, "He'd like a picture. Can you give me the camera?" I groaned inwardly, but the older daughter of Adrian/Hadrian fame pointed out that I wanted a picture on my phone. I handed it over with low expectations, and she took only one shot. But it turned out very well, and I did not have to rely on a selfie at the end of the trek.

They moved on, and I sat again for what was indeed my solo moment. I stamped the passport, gazed at the wide expanse of the beach below the

Banks leading to the firth. There were gulls and maybe other birds flocked down there, but I couldn't identify them and didn't have the energy at this point to try too hard.

I was preparing to think about departure to the local pub when three young women in their twenties, very fit, ran up to finish their journey on the path. We chatted a bit. They had run the trail in four days, a thing they liked to do at various historical or famous trails on long weekends around England and Europe. I was quite impressed. Even better, they had a car hired for the journey back to Carlisle. Even though they were on a different train to London, this saved my hide. As it turned out, there was no way I could have gotten a taxi at that point since I didn't book ahead, and it was the bank holiday. Nor did I have lodgings in Bowness— and I wasn't eager to see the Dutchmen over dinner anyway. They agreed I could join them and share in the fare. We then walked to the pub for refreshments, where the driver was due to meet them in an hour. Gentlemanly, I let them go first because I knew they would be much faster than I with pack and sore feet. Over drinks and crisps, we shared a few stories of our walks. The only one I clearly remember was their experience of the diversion in Carlisle after the park, which had forced me to the city center and the cab ride. They had breezed through that morning while the workers were repairing the bridge that had been closed to me the day before.

I was somewhat in awe of their speed-walking over 20 miles a day, especially on the crags and cliffs around the Pennines, where I had followed Clayton's Wall with Anne and Ginna four days ago. Soon we were in the hired car. I had to sit backward on the jump seat facing them, which I almost never did as a child in station wagons because I would throw up upon exiting the car, but this time it worked out fine, and soon we were in Carlisle at the train station. We parted company. I had time for a proper lunch and found a pub, where I had some very poor, dried-out fish and chips. I then struggled over to the platform and my train to London Euston. Thank God I didn't have to change trains.

And thank God I had made a seat reservation before catching the train to Newcastle nine days before. The train was packed; we were the proverbial sardines. Aisles were clogged and the spaces between cars full of folks sitting if possible, standing if not. There was barely room to move, and I had to hold on to my pack much of the way. Somehow I changed to my sandals and went to the loo once. Surprisingly, I never slept, although there wasn't much room or peace and quiet.

When I arrived in London, all the joints had stiffened up again and I could barely walk. It was much worse than the morning. Anne and Ginna were in a garden apartment over in Hammersmith, west London, so I had a thirty-minute tube journey. It was very crowded in Euston Station at the end of the bank holiday as people returned to London. I was blocking a considerable amount of walkway, with pack and poles now swinging from the back, and I was walking at a pace more suited to an octogenarian. I made it slowly to the underground station at Euston, but to be honest, I don't remember the tube ride that followed. I exited at Hammersmith, a very large underground station with a shopping mall and, mercifully, escalators. I pulled my phone out for directions and stumbled along the streets for a bit over a quarter-mile to our apartment, with of course one last wrong turn. I messed up the entry code a few times with my shaky hands before I could get in the flat to find Anne and Ginna and a warm welcome for the successful walker.

They had assumed I would be both tired and hungry, which was true, although more tired and sore than hungry. They also assumed I wouldn't want to spend a lot of time deciding on a restaurant, so they had chosen one ahead of time. Once I dropped my gear and had a soak—we had chosen a rental with a hot tub—we set off for a pizza place that was close by and had good reviews. Well, it was close for them. I couldn't keep up, which is when Ginna called me a drama queen. I protested that this was way more than drama. They hadn't seen the blisters, so they slowed way down for me, and we had a very nice meal. I think this was the only meal of the trip, perhaps the only meal ever in London or Europe, where I didn't take pictures.

We walked slowly back in the dark of west London to the garden apartment. A fox strolled by at one point on one of the darker Hammersmith streets. The flat was at the bottom of a central skylight with a small courtyard, open to the sky. It rained all night and I awoke, stiff and sore, to the sound of dripping eaves early in the London dawn.

The night before, I sat in that beautiful room at Hillside Farm on Bousted Hill after Sandra had picked me up at the pub, watching the sun set over Scotland. This was my true moment of triumph. My sore feet were resting on the windowsill. I had a glass of wine and a beautiful view over the marshy field to the river and its wide banks. The waters still shimmered at first in the glow of the sun, heading back across the Atlantic to my home in Indiana. Purple clouds, flat as anvils and long across the horizon, slowly became darker, etched in blues as the sun finally set. The travails and pains of the next day, yet unknown, were ahead of me. I was happy. I had done it.

And then, the next day, it was over. For a week, two weeks, three weeks, I lived in the moment. Reliving the routes and photos and researching Hadrian and the wall was my work as I prepared the lecture. But soon life intervened—deadlines, meetings, another trip, the daily grind. Experience faded to memory.

This is how we experience a death. The loved one is there, in the house, in class, at work, always available on the phone. And then he's not. For a while, for a parent or close friend, he stays alive in your heart, in your experience. You can feel him. But experience soon fades to memory, and memories dim. He's alive in photographs and stories from time to time. But he's gone.

I remember talking to my therapist two weeks after his death, a young intern who had started counseling me at the University Health Center in April after the first suicide attempt. At the end of the session he said, "In one hour you have expressed anger, pain, love, and pride in your father. All of this is in there."

Experience with death brings compassion. When my brother died at age twenty in a car accident, Peter Lee, then Rector of the Chapel of the Cross in Chapel Hill, told me I had changed because now I understood what it was like to experience sudden death of a family member. Some years ago, during communion at church, I looked over to see a family gathered at the altar rail after the death of their mother the night before. We had watched this woman's Alzheimer's disease progress the autumn before, her well-dressed, patient husband bringing her every Sunday. This was during the time when Anne and her sister were helping their mother move into a memory care facility, so sitting nearby was very painful for her. One Sunday a few months ago, the woman was gone and then she died. When I saw the family at communion, I started to cry while kneeling at the rail. And I was crying for myself as well as them.

A few months after the walk across Hadrian's Wall, as twenty-five years became twenty-five years and three months, I realized while walking the dog by the creek that I would never have a conversation with my father. That seems obvious, of course, hardly unique to me. Indeed, that acute realization is one of the most painful parts of grief when a loved one dies. But memories fade, one year becomes five, ten, and now twenty-five. Experience fades and becomes memory. Memory becomes narrative.

I had started a conversation. I realized with new clarity after that walk in August that the conversation was one-way.

EPILOGUE

gave my LaFollette Lecture as planned, five months after the walk. People seemed to like it, and I received a lot of nice compliments, although no one as far as I can remember stood up to cheer, despite my daydreams in the saddle the year before of a standing ovation. Reality tempered enthusiasm, which resulted in a less ambitious lecture, but one that I think was a lot easier to listen to. People laughed at all the jokes, including the one about Hadrian building a wall and making the Britons pay for it, which was gratifying. It was funny. There was a bit of tension in the room when I introduced Antinous; I'm not sure how many same-sex relationships have been featured in LaFollette Lectures over the years— maybe once before with Plato's *Symposium*. But when I turned to Dad, you could have heard a pin drop. They laughed out of relief in the second half at any joke after I started talking about my father. I got a lot of hugs afterward from family and colleagues, who were suddenly closer friends.

My mother was there, and she understood it all, which was one of my goals; I didn't want to give an obtuse, academic talk for the handful of specialists in the room. My older sister, Beth, as well, and our son, Nolen, and of course Anne; Ginna was studying abroad in Spain. I offered copies to both Mom and Beth the day before. My mother chose to read it, to be ready, while Beth said she was ready and would read it afterward. I don't think either of them cried. The lecture was at 4:45 p.m. on a Friday afternoon, after a Trustees' Meeting, since they usually attend. I practiced the entire lecture in the empty hall at about 2:00 and almost broke down when I talked about my father. I was worried, but I made it through the real lecture with a quavering voice and, for me, fairly poor delivery. I also had a problem with the remote control for my slides. One of my students said to me afterward, about my walking over to the computer to advance the slide when my remote control didn't work: "bend don't break!" I know my voice was off because I watched the video online and then, a few weeks after the lecture, was interviewed on campus by a colleague in communications and marketing. He, Rich, had gone on a trip with my class to Israel and Palestine just a few weeks earlier, at Thanksgiving break, a month after the lecture. We talked about the trip, the lecture, walking, food, all sorts of things. You can listen to my voice online for both the lecture and the podcast; the way I sound is so different, like night and day. Opening up in front of 250 people after twenty-five years of relative silence was hard. But now it has become easier as I open up to you and everyone reading this book.

The title of the lecture was Walking Hadrian's Wall: Meditations on Romans, Christians, Birds, and Growing Older. Romans and Christians should be obvious; my professional life has focused on studying early Christians in the Roman Empire, and I've written two books and many articles on the New Testament and early Christianity. And, as you already have learned, I am indeed an avid birder. I also thought they made a whimsical placeholder to signal that the talk would be about more than the history of Hadrian's Wall or early Christianity. The birds stood for life in general, but I thought Meditations on Romans, Christians, and Life would make a terrible subtitle. As it turned out, I saw forty-four different species during the walk, a nice number, and five of them were new birds or "lifers" for me. But this was not as many as I thought I might see, walking hours and hours through the countryside for nine days and over 100 miles. I found that trekking with a pack and being absorbed in the wall, the history of the artifact, and self-reflection divided my attention from just focusing on birds. It takes time to bird, and as you now know, I was often short on time. Only the kittiwakes made the lecture.

That December, two months after the lecture, I traveled to Rome to learn more about Hadrian. I spent a lot of time at his Pantheon (got there early in the morning when it was empty) and a day studying the ruins of his enormous villa in Tivoli, where the ruins of the Antinoeion lie as well as many other fantastic structures. On the last day in Rome, before flying to Spain where I would meet up with Anne and then Ginna after her semester abroad, I went to see Hadrian's mausoleum.

You might know this as Castel Sant'Angelo, the structure with a secret passageway from the Vatican for popes to escape. It was featured in Dan Brown's *Angels and Demons,* a book and film I enjoyed very much. Sitting across the Tiber River from the center of Rome, it is not far from Vatican City. This is because in Roman times tombs had to be outside the city. If you visit Rome, you can walk along the ancient Via Latina or Via Appia and find tombs and catacombs. But Hadrian, as usual, did things differently. He built the largest tomb ever in Rome, right across the Tiber, visible from the Campus Martius and much of Rome, almost but not quite across from Augustus's smaller mausoleum. He even built a bridge for Romans to use to come see the tombs of the Great Emperor and God Hadrian and his family, including a few later emperors wanting to associate their line with Hadrian. It's an imposing structure, at one point the tallest building in Rome, with sweeping views of the Tiber and the piazza and basilica of St. Peter's, only a ten-minute walk away. There's not much of Hadrian left here, some Roman pieces of the old façade and niches for urns and colossal statues. There is a nice model of what it used to look like, with pilasters and hundreds of statues around the roof line. Hadrian had a *quadriga*, a four-horse Olympic chariot, on the peak of the top. Since medieval times, a statue of the archangel Michael has stood there, giving Castel Sant'Angelo its name.

When my father died, he was cremated, like my brother before him, and his ashes were placed in the new columbarium at St. Anne's, my family church in Atlanta. I went over to the church that week when I learned they were there but they had already been buried. I dug them up and buried them again, by myself.

Twenty-five years later, I dug that grave up again and sifted through all the ashes of my thirty years with my father, all the pain, all the loss. Twenty-five years later, I opened up that grave one more time. I looked through everything in there, thirty years of my life, fifty-eight of his. And now, I've closed it again one last time. I've buried it and laid him to rest. *Requiescat in Pace.*

ABOUT THE AUTHOR

 Bob Royalty is Professor of History and Religion at Wabash College in Crawfordsville, Indiana. Raised in Atlanta, he attended the University of North Carolina at Chapel Hill, Yale Divinity School, and Yale University Graduate School. He is the author of two scholarly monographs (*The Streets of Heaven*, Mercer University Press, 1996; and *The Origin of Heresy*, Routledge, 2013) and numerous articles and reference entries. He and his spouse, Anne, divide their time between homes in Indiana and North Carolina. Their two grown children live in New York City.